Companion book to the exhibition
The return of the Lion Man
History Myth Magic
Ulmer Museum
November 15, 2013 – June 9, 2014

A project of the Ulmer Museum
and the State Office for the
Preservation of Historical Monuments,
Regional Council Stuttgart

Stadt Ulm
Ulmer Museum

Baden-Württemberg
LANDESAMT FÜR DENKMALPFLEGE
IM REGIERUNGSPRÄSIDIUM STUTTGART

Greeting
Prof. Dr. Dirk Krausse, State archeologist/State conservator
State Office for the Preservation of Historical Monuments,
Regional Council Stuttgart

Baden-Württemberg is among the most archeologically rich landscapes in Germany and Central Europe. Paleolithic caves, stilt houses or pile dwellings from the Neolithic and Bronze Age, early Celtic princely tombs or the Roman Limes – all of these archeological treasures were buried in the ground beneath Southwestern Germany. The probably most significant archeological find from Baden-Württemberg – from the point of view of world history – is the Lion Man from the Hohlenstein. He towers over the other pieces of Ice Age art – physically as well as figuratively – because to his size and his representation, the blending of animal and man. The Lion Man is unique evidence for the development of human thought and imagination.

The Lion Man has become very popular with (international) audiences in recent years. This is in part due to the sensational discovery of additional fragments, discovered during excavations by the State Office for the Preservation of Historical Monuments Baden-Württemberg in the Lone Valley, which could be refit to the original statuette. These new finds provided the impulse for a renewed restoration that was carried out in 2012/13 in the workshop of the State Office for the Preservation of Historical Monuments by a team under the leadership of Prof. Dr. Claus-Joachim Kind and Dipl.-Rest. Nicole Ebinger-Rist, including

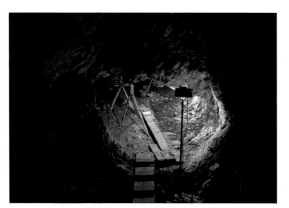

Anette Lerch and Sibylle Wolf. The Ministry for Finance and Economics of the State of Baden-Württemberg supported the project financially. We are pleased that the more complete and restored Lion Man has finally returned to the Ulmer Museum and we wish him many visitors from around the world!

Foreword
Dr. Gabriele Holthuis, Director Ulmer Museum
Kurt Wehrberger M.A., Curator Archaeology Ulmer Museum

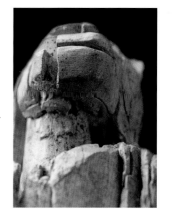

The small sculptures made out of mammoth ivory – between 40,000 and 35,000 years old – from the caves of the Swabian Jura near Ulm are the oldest pieces of figurative art made by human kind. The largest and most fascinating of these figures is the Lion Man.

A team of archeologists from the State Office for the Preservation of Historical Monuments Baden-Württemberg (Landesamt für Denkmalpflege Baden-Württemberg) carried out new excavations in the Hohlenstein-Stadel cave in the Lone Valley and, in 2009, surprisingly rediscovered the original place, where the statuette had been found in the course of 1939 excavations. The following excavations saw the find of many more important pieces from the Lion Man. They were left behind in the cave after the first excavation came to an abrupt end only days prior to the start of the Second World War. These pieces helped to get the fragmentary statuette more complete. During an extensive restoration process hundreds of fragments were fit together with pieces that could previously not be attached to the statuette and had been stored at the museum. It is now a bit larger and more details of the figure have become visible.

The Ulmer Museum saw the "Return of the Lion Man" as an opportunity to create a special exhibition highlighting the statuette. It focuses on the mysterious and fascinating story of its discovery and exploration as well as on its significance within the context of the development of art and culture.

We would like to thank all of the people and institutions that supported and helped to bring this joint project of the Ulmer Museum and State Office for the Preservation of Historical Monuments Baden-Württemberg to a successful conclusion. Special thanks go to the archeological restoration-workshop of the State Office whose incredibly complex restoration of the statuette laid the groundwork for this exhibition. Numerous colleagues from the State Office, the University of Tübingen and other institutions as well as private individuals also supported us in preparation for the exhibition. The book was only made possible through the cooperation of competent colleagues. At this point, we would like to express our sincere thanks to all of the participating authors. The creative implementation of the exhibition and the book was placed into the hands of Braun Engels Gestaltung (Ulm).

Thanks is also due to our lenders who made available to us for the presentation in Ulm pieces that are rarely put on display. And finally, we would like to thank the city of Ulm for its generous financial support of the exhibition as well as our patrons, without whose contributions the realization of the exhibition and the current book would not have been possible in this form.

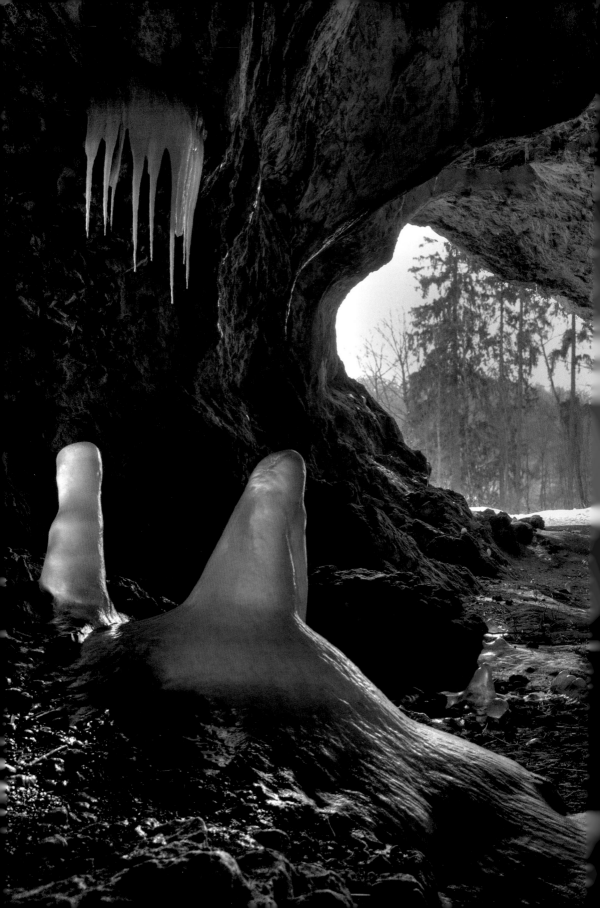

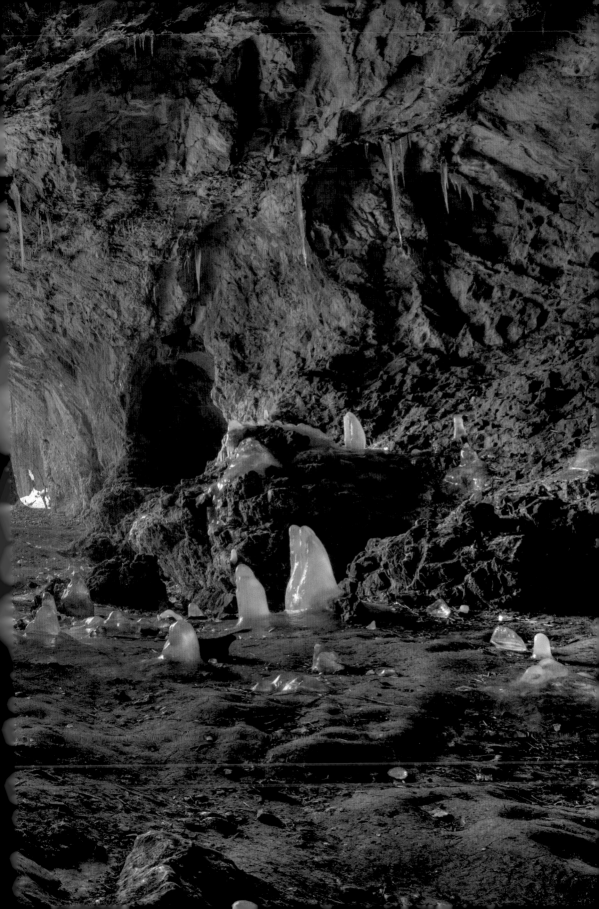

AN EL DORADO FOR STONE AGE EXPLORERS

THE SWABIAN JURA
KURT WEHRBERGER

1 The Bockstein cave in the Lone Valley. Watercolor from a publication by Ludwig Bürger, 1892 **2** Oscar Fraas (1824–1897). Portrait from 1880 **3** Robert Rudolf Schmidt (1882–1950), Founder and head of the Prehistoric Institute at the University of Tübingen from 1921–1929 **4** The Hohle Fels in the Ach Valley in the 19th century. Wood engraving from a publication by Oscar Fraas, 1872

"Humans – contemporaries of mammoths and cave bears!" This was a bold statement in the middle of the 19th century and often resulted in fierce discussions. In Southern Germany, the geologist and paleontologist Oscar Fraas (1824–1897) was first able to prove the coexistence of humans and Ice Age animals through the discovery of a reindeer hunting camp near the source of river Schussen on the banks of the Federsee marsh in 1866. In 1861, Fraas had discovered similar evidence at a cave in the rocky massif of the Hohlenstein in the Lone Valley. In his eagerness to search for the remains of cave bears – he reported 10,000 bones from 400 animals – he missed the carefully produced tools and pieces of jewelry, fashioned by human hands. Later, Fraas returned to the Lone Valley and recovered numerous overlooked artifacts from the previously excavated sediments. In the following years, specialist and interested layman sought out additional caves; one of these was the Hohle Fels in the Ach Valley. The cave deposits contained a large amount of bat dung which was sold as fertilizer

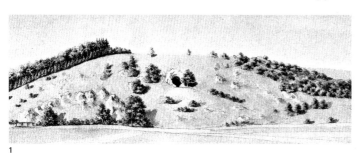

1

("Swabian Guano"). The bear bones that were found during this harvest were sold to collectors. Excavations in the cave in 1870/71 by Fraas together with the preacher Theodor Hartmann (1829–1885) brought to light a large amount of ice-aged animal bones as well as tools and jewelry made out of stone, bone and antler.

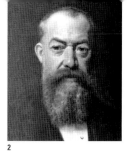

2

In 1883/84, the forest ranger Ludwig Bürger from Langenau (1844–1898) excavated the Bockstein cave in the Lone Valley with similar success. The discovery of the grave of a woman and a child in the Bockstein cave sparked a severe dispute. Well-known scholars declared that the grave was recent and it was not until 1997 that scientific dating methods were able to place the time of death into the 7th millenium B.C.

In 1906, Robert Rudolf Schmidt (1882–1950), the later founder of the Institute for Prehistory (Urgeschichtliches Forschungsinstitut) at the University of Tübingen, explored the Sirgenstein cave in the Ach Valley – in the 15th century, the Dominican monk Felix Fabri from Ulm had described the cave as the home of Cyclops. Schmidt first recognized that the superimposed sedimentary layers represented a sequence of prehistoric cultural horizons. Exemplary for the caves of the Swabian Jura, he correlated these with the Paleolithic cultures of France. Although later excavations worked to correct this picture, parts of his system are still valid today. The pre-historic archaeology of Central Europe still utilizes French terminology to describe past cultures. Thus the culture from the begin of the Upper Paleolithic, the Aurigna-cian, is named after the find site Aurignac in the foreland of the Pyrenees.

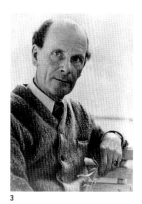

3

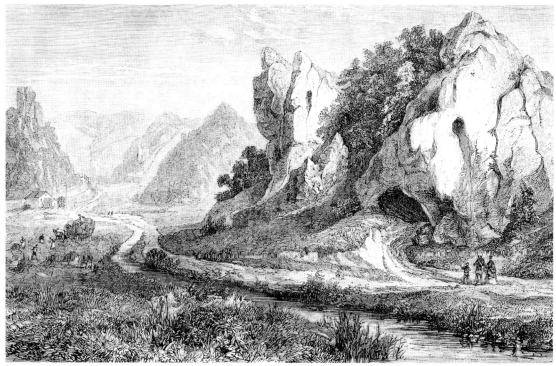

4

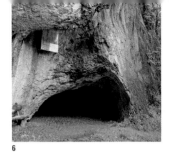

6

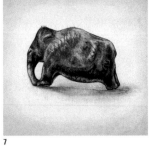

7

5 Southwest entrance to the Vogelherd cave   **6** The Sirgenstein in the Ach Valley   **7** The mammoth, one of the most famous ivory figurines from the Vogelherd cave. Drawing from the publication by Gustav Riek in 1934   **8** Vogelherd. The southwestern entrance at the start of the excavations in the summer of 1931

In 1908, Schmidt, after undertaking sample excavations at the Bockstein cave previously explored by Bürger, excavated at the Kleine Scheuer, a rockshelter between the Stadel and the Bärenhöhle at the Hohlenstein in the Lone Valley. The late glacial layers, excavated subsequently in small campaigns at last in 1974, brought to light a rich faunal assemblage with more than 30 different species of animal that document the climate change towards the end of the Ice Age. In 1913, excavations at the Kogelstein near Schelklingen in the Ach Valley unearthed evidence of a Neanderthal resting place. New excavations carried out by the State Office for the Preservation of Historical Monuments in 1987 and 1996 identified the site as a collapsed cave.

1931
FANFARE AT THE VOGELHERD

In 1931, a badger's burrow led to the discovery of a so far unknown cave. The expelled sediments contained flint splinters, which caused the geologist Gustav Riek (1900–1976), at this time assistant at the Institute for Prehistory at the University of Tübingen, to excavate the entire cave within three months. The small ivory figurines that he discovered in the layers from the early Upper Paleolithic caused quite a stir. Riek recovered about a dozen fragmentary figurines depicting ice-aged fauna such as mammoth, wild horse and cave lion. It was the first time that excavations of the Swabian caves recovered evidence for artistic expression of the highest quality except of the typical weapons, tools and jewelry. The remains of two human skulls were originally believed to be as old as the other finds, however, recent scientific dating methods proved that they were only a few thousand years old and originate from an occupation of the cave during the Neolithic.

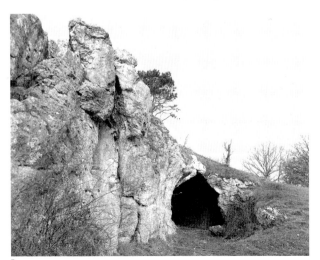

5

After excavating the Vogelherd cave, Gustav Riek also explored the Burkhardtshöhle at the northern ridge of the Jura (1933/34) and the cave ruin Haldenstein near the source of the Lone River (1936). In 1932, the anatomist and prehistoric explorer from Tübingen Robert Wetzel (1898–1962) started excavations at the Bockstein massif in the Lone Valley. He uncovered a resting

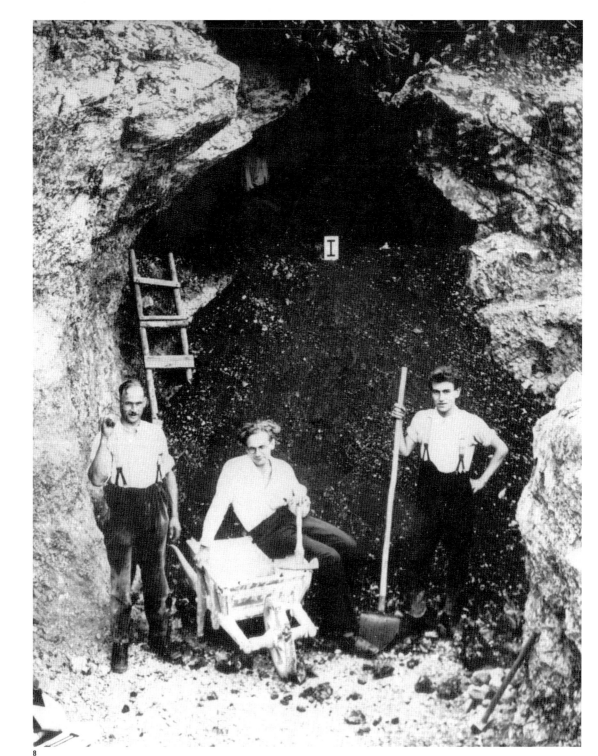

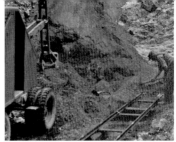

11

area from the era of the Neanderthals, ca. 60,000 years old, called Bockstein-schmiede, located near to the Bockstein cave. After this success, Wetzel moved 2 km down the valley to the Hohlenstein where he systematically excavated the Stadel cave from 1937 to 1939 after a sample excavation in 1935.

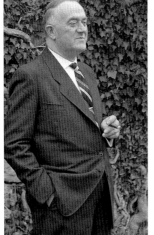

9

AFTER THE WAR
IN THE ACH AND LONE VALLEY

Cave archeology on the Swabian Jura was put on hold during World War II and in the postwar period. It wasn't until the mid-fifties that Gustav Riek and Robert Wetzel recommenced their work. Riek transferred his focus to the area around Blaubeuren in the Ach Valley where he consequently excavated the Brillen-

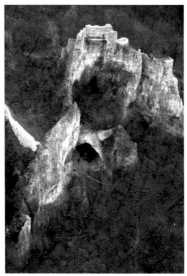

höhle (1955–1963) and the Große Grotte (1959–1964). The Brillenhöhle, named after two collapsed holes in the cave ceiling, contained multiple layers from the Upper Paleolithic; the Große Grotte contained finds from the era of the Neanderthals. Riek also undertook smaller excavations at the Hohle Fels and the Helga-Abri (1958–1960) located to the west of this cave.

Wetzel continued working at the Bock-stein in 1953. He wanted to realize his vision from before the war: To reconstruct the history of a small region, in this case the Lone Valley, through the past tens of thousands of years. Although he was not

10

successful, the collaboration with different scientific disciplines – geology, botany and zoology – to clarify climatic and cultural developments during the last Ice Age, was progressive for the time period. While excavating at the Bockstein, Wetzel also turned his attention to the caves of the Hohlenstein. From 1954 to 1961 he conducted annual explorations, with the exception of the year 1958, of the Stadel cave. He also explored the Bärenhöhle during this period. With Wetzel's death in 1962 also came the temporary end of archeological exploration in the Lone Valley.

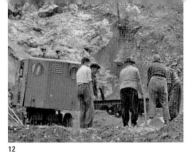
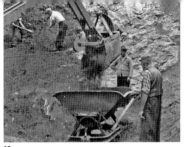

12   13

PILOT PROJECT GEISSENKLÖSTERLE
THE PATH TO MODERN CAVE ARCHEOLOGY

The excavation of the Geißenklösterle cave from 1974 to 1991 under the direction of Joachim Hahn (1942–1997) set new standards for excavation techniques, documentation and analysis. The cave ruin is located 60 m above the Ach Valley floor and was first identified as a prehistoric find site in 1957. Picks and shovels were a thing of the past! Hahn adapted the French, more precise methods of excavation:

9 Gustav Riek (1900–1976)   **10** Große Grotte with the medieval castle ruin Hohengerhausen (Rusenschloss) at the eastern rim of the Blaubeuren basin **11–14** Bockstein 1956. Excavations with heavy machinery on the ridge below the Bocksteinschmiede. Photos from Robert Wetzel's diary

Thinner layers were removed using smaller tools and following natural sediment strata, the excavated surface was divided into square meters, the square meters into quarters, and the resulting sediments were washed and sieved. These methods allow the excavator to recognize small archaeological finds that are not always visible at first glance as well as the bones of smaller animals that found their way into the cave without human help, e.g. through the pellets from birds of prey.

While working at the Geißenklösterle, Hahn completed his excavation of the Helga-Abri and, in 1997, more than 100 years after Oscar Fraas, began exploration of the Hohle Fels cave. These excavations have continued since then under the direction of Nicholas J. Conard from the Institute for Prehistory at the University of Tübingen.

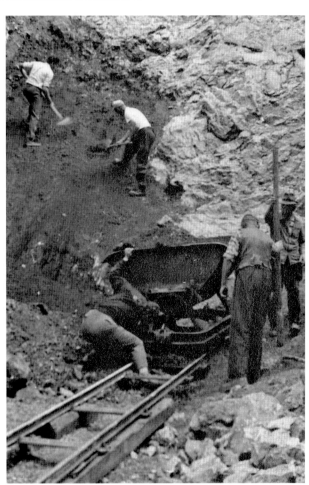

14

Neue Höhlen ausgegraben
Tübinger Urgeschichtler suchen nach weiteren Zeugnissen der Eiszeitkunst

15

Alongside his research at the Hohle Fels, Conard undertook new archeological excavations in the vicinity of the Vogelherd cave in the Lone Valley since 2005; the campaigns lasted several weeks and took place annually until 2012. The goal was to reanalyze the sediments from Riek's 1931 excavation; as a result, numerous previously overlooked artifacts were recovered. The Hohlenstein had not been the focus of archeological research since Robert Wetzel's last excavation in 1961 – with the exception of a sample excavation at the Stadel cave in 1983 and smaller explorations below the cave entrance and in the floodplain in 1997/98. Archeologist turned their attention to this cave as a result of the preparation of an application to have the four "Swabian" caves with Paleolithic art added to the UNESCO World Heritage List. Claus-Joachim Kind from State Office for the Preservation of Historical Monuments Baden-Württemberg directed the new excavations at the Stadel cave between 2008 and 2013.

FORGOTTEN AND BURIED
CAVE EXPLORATION IN THE LONE VALLEY

"Somewhere near the Hohlenstein rock lies the Teufelsloch or Teufelsküche, a cave that we haven't been able to locate". In fact, years after this note in a description of monuments from 1961, it has not been possible to identify which

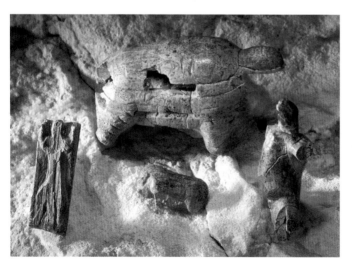

of the numerous small, nameless rock openings or rock shelters in the Lone Valley is this cave, named by Oscar Fraas after he found numerous flint splinters there during prospects in the 1860s. Some believe that the cave is located southwest of the Hohlenstein, others believe to have identified its location to the southeast of the rock massif.

16

In 2013, archeologists from the University of Tübingen began the search for additional buried caves in the Lone Valley. The groundwork was laid by a biologist – just as forest rangers, hunters or local historians once helped to discover the Bärenhöhle at the Hohlenstein (1861), the Vogelherd cave (1931) or the Bockstein-schmiede (1932) – who followed the tracks of animals such as fox or badger who prefer to use natural caves and caverns for the construction of their burrows in the rocky slopes. A systematic search in the past winter led to the discovery of around 50 sites that may lead to buried caves.

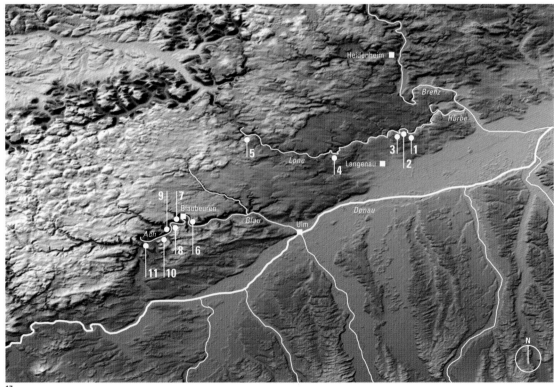

17

1	Vogelherd	5	Haldenstein
2	Hohlenstein	6	Große Grotte
	(Stadel, Bärenhöhle,	7	Brillenhöhle
	Kleine Scheuer)	8	Geißenklösterle
3	Bockstein-Complex	9	Sirgenstein
	with Bocksteinhöhle and	10	Hohle Fels
	Bocksteinschmiede	11	Kogelstein
4	Fohlenhaus		

18 Vogelherd. Fish (2008), ivory, L 7.0 cm
19 Vogelherd. Lion (1931) with head
(2012), ivory, L 8.3 cm **20** Vogelherd.
Lion (2006), ivory, L 5.6 cm **21** Vogelherd. Mammoth in the backdirt (2006)
22 Vogelherd. Personal ornaments and
organic tools from the re-excavation

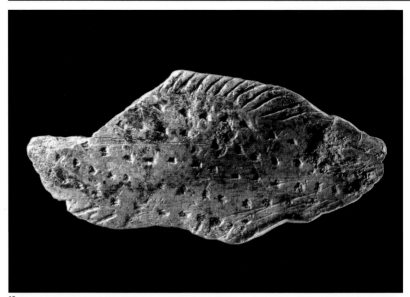

18

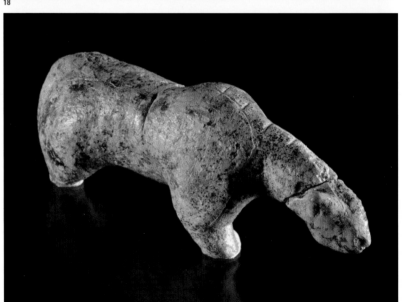

19

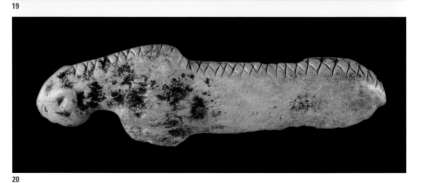

20

Nicholas J. Conard

Vogelherd is the richest of all the Aurignacian sites of the Swabian Jura and perhaps also the best known. The site was discovered in the spring of 1931 by Hermann Mohn and excavated by a team under the direction of Gustav Riek from the University of Tübingen over a period of about 12 weeks in the summer of the same year. Riek's excavation proceeded at a speed much faster than modern fieldwork, but the high quality results from the excavation indicate that the dig was executed with great care. The original excavation produced finds from the entire spectrum of Aurignacian material culture with vast numbers of organic artifacts, faunal remains and lithic artifacts from this period, in addition to far lesser amounts of finds from the proceeding Middle Paleolithic and the later phases of the Upper Paleolithic. The site also preserved finds from the

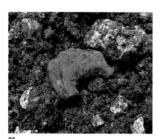

Neolithic, most notably the famous human skeletal remains, which Riek originally attributed to the early Aurignacian. While the site is known for many reasons, the recovery of nearly a dozen examples exquisitely

carved small figurines of mammoth ivory have counted among the great masterpieces of Ice Age art since their discovery. In the decades following the excavation in 1931 various legal und illegial digs took place at the site. In the years leading up to the Baden-Württemberg state exhibit on the art and culture of the Ice Age in 2009, the author undertook a systematic excavation of the back-dirt from Riek's fieldwork. The project took longer than originally expected, and all eight excavation seasons from 2005–2012 were needed to complete the re-excavation. The work was well worth the effort with numerous new finds of Aurignacian art being re-covered including depictions of mammoths, lions, fish and many other depictions that are harder to identify to a specific species. The new phase of excavation also recovered fragments of flutes made from mammoth ivory and a bird bone. Additionally, several hundred examples of small ivory ornaments have been recovered. The original excavation produced none of these important finds. The sorting and refitting of the new finds is still underway, but our preliminary results suggest that many more discoveries lie ahead as the more than 32,000 samples from the re-excavation at Vogel-herd are systematically studied.

In May 2013 the Archäopark Vogelherd opened. Located directly at the site, the park offers many opportunities to explore Ice Age life. The complete depiction of the mammoth from 2006 represents the highlight of the exhibit.

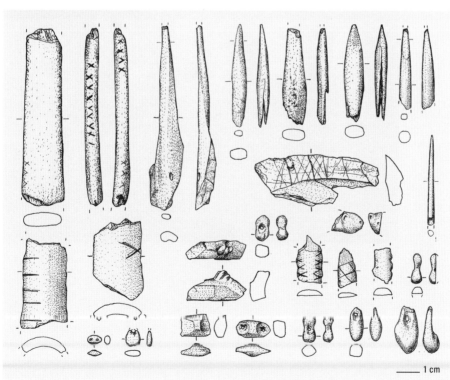

—— 1 cm

23 Hohle Fels. Personal ornaments from the Aurignacian   **24** Hohle Fels. View of the recent excavations   **25** Hohle Fels. Waterbird, ivory, L 4.7 cm

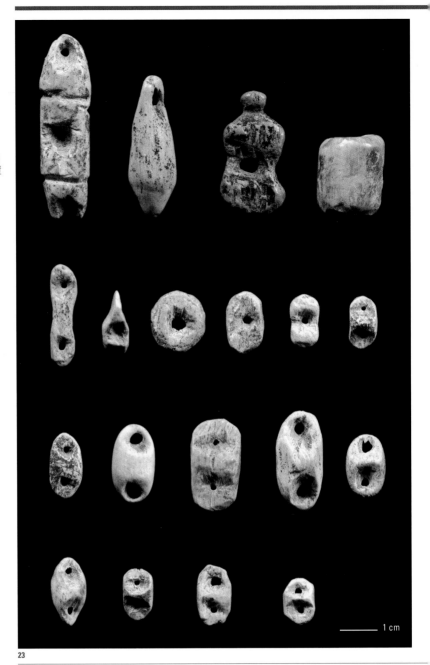

23

Nicholas J. Conard

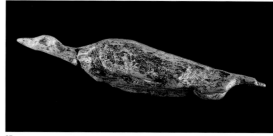

25

Hohle Fels near the town of Schelklingen in the Ach Valley west of Ulm has long and illustrious history of research and is one of the best known caves of the Swabian Jura. The first Paleolithic artifacts were discovered at the site during excavations by Oscar Fraas and Theodor Hartmann in 1870 and 1871. This work led to the recovery of lithic and organic artifacts from the Upper Paleolithic and vast amounts of cave bear bones and other paleontological remains. Later excavations by Gustav Riek between 1958 and 1960 and by Joachim Hahn most years from 1977–1996 led to the recovery of important assemblages from the Gravettian and Magdalenian phases of the Upper Paleolithic.

Starting in 1997 the author began excavations at the site. This work, which has proceeded annually for each of the last 17 summers, has led to the extension of the excavation in the Gravettian and Magdalenian deposits as well as to the discovery of many new find horizons dating to the Middle Paleolithic and the Aurignacian. These cultural periods reflects the later part of the era during which Neanderthals lived in Europe and the period in which modern humans arrived in Europe. The caves of the Swabian Jura preserve a uniquely rich record of this key phase of human history.

The Middle Paleolithic occupation of Hohle Fels is characterized by low levels of occupational intensity that reflect repeated short-term stays at the site by Neanderthals. Following an occupational hiatus, around roughly 42,000 years ago modern humans arrived in the Ach Valley. They presumably arrived via the Danube and quickly established stable populations in the region. At Hohle Fels, as at most other sites in the region, the Aurignacian deposits are much richer in all classes of finds than are those of the Middle Paleolithic.

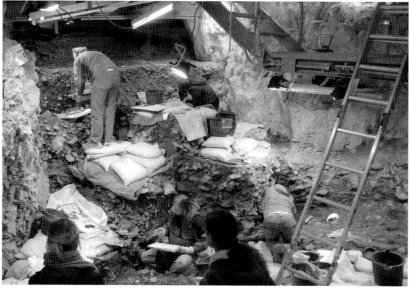

Studies of seasonality suggest that site was occupied in the cold months of the year when conditions in the open-air would have been particularly harsh. The recent phases of excavation have produced important materials from all of the periods the cave was used, but Hohle Fels is probably best known for the discovery of a number of carved ivory figurines and the remains of three flutes that date to the early Aurignacian.

UNDER THE SIGN OF THE SWASTIKA

LONE VALLEY EXCAVATIONS DURING THE NATIONAL SOCIALIST REGIME

KURT WEHRBERGER

In 1931 news of the sensational finds from Gustav Riek's excavation at the Vogelherd cave reached Robert Wetzel, born in Tübingen, who taught at the University of Würzburg at this time and who would later take up the post as director of the Institute for Anatomy in Tübingen in 1936. They nourished his dreams to search for

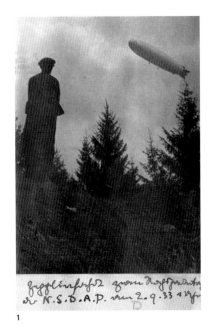

1

and find additional caves in the Lone Valley by his own. It was an advantage that he was able to employ some of the workers who had previously worked for Riek during the excavation at the Vogelherd, specifically Anton Bamberger who was very familiar with the environs of the Lone Valley. Therefore it was not a coincidence that he chose to investigate the Bockstein massif, the location of the Bockstein cave with the early Paleolithic settlement site discovered in the 19th century. His excavations were quickly crowned with success: West of the cave he discovered the Bocksteinschmiede, a site with rich finds from the time of Neanderthals. Wetzel leased the property from the city of Öllingen and was granted ownership and disposal rights for any finds he discovered there. He was granted permission to excavate by the State Office for Preservation of Historical Monuments at Stuttgart. During this early research period between 1932 and 1935, Wetzel's enthusiasm for national socialist ideas in combination with archeological research became more and more apparent. One question that drove him was whether the Germans could trace their roots back to ice-aged hunters.

In 1935, Wetzel turned his attention to the Stadel cave at the Hohlenstein. A test excavation in the cave, where Robert Rudolf Schmidt had previously excavated a test trench, showed that the cave contained early Paleolithic layers. Scheduled excavations took place from 1937 to 1939. The geologist Otto Völzing led the excavation on site; Wetzel was rarely seen at the excavation site. He had been named vice-rector of the university and was the director of the National Socialist University Teachers' League (NSD-Dozentenbund) and used his power to actively implement the national socialist ideology at the University of Tübingen.

The systematic excavation in the Stadel cave was closely related to Wetzel's political activities. He secured the assistance of the "Ahnenerbe" organization, founded in 1935 by the Reichsführer SS Heinrich Himmler (1900–1945), for his archeological activities. In the fall of 1935, Himmler accepted Wetzel's "Lontalplan" and took over the patronage of the Stadel excavation. The proposal, written by Wetzel, Völzing, the anthropologist and director of the Institute for Racial Studies at the University of Tübingen Wilhelm Gieseler (1900–1976) and the medical man Karl Keller (1914–1987), and supplemented by a temporary report on the results of the excavation, was not published until 1941, long after research at the cave had been closed down due to the war. When Himmler announced that he would visit the Lone Valley in 1939, Wetzel ordered that the test excavation from the previous year be turned into a presentable excavation. This was abandoned

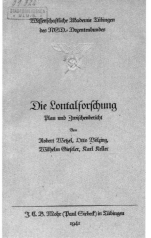

3

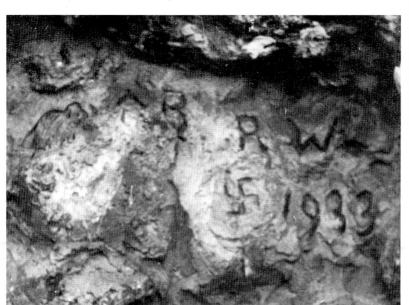

2

4 Excavation on the terrace in front of the Stadel cave in 1937 **5** Robert Wetzel (1898–1962) signing finds in front of the Hohlenstein 1960

shortly after when the Reichsführer SS cancelled his visit. After the start of systematic excavations at the Stadel cave in 1937, the SS flag was raised at times above the excavation to show that the "Ahnenerbe" supported the project and also men from the SS assembly house in Tübingen worked at the site.

Wetzel's research was initially supported by Gustav Riek who had joined the NSDAP in 1929 and was, like Wetzel, a member of the SS as first lieutenant of the SS. Wetzel and Riek were united against Hans Reinerth (1900–1990), director of the "Reichsbund für Vorgeschichte", who organized a conference in 1936 in Ulm with an impressive 3,000 participants, the majority of whom were history teachers from the NS teacher's league. Reinerth, whose Reichsbund belonged to "Einsatzstab Reichsleiter Rosenberg", NSDAP chief ideologist Alfred Rosenberg (1893–1946), heavily criticized the prehistoric research in Württemberg in the hope of gaining supremacy over all the archeological excavations in the region. Riek and

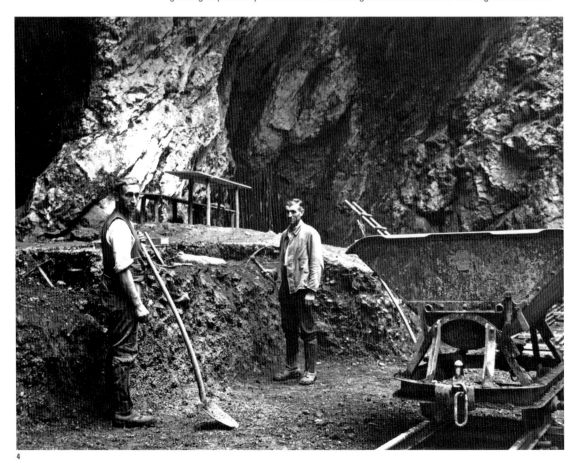

4

Robert Wetzel: Anatomist, prehistorian and national socialist

Philip Scharer

Robert Wetzel was born in 1898 in Tübingen, a university town in Swabia. His interest in prehistory was aroused during childhood: In 1908, ten-year old Robert found numerous fossils in the foundation pit of the summerhouse that his parents were building in Tübingen-Bebenhausen. Thus began his decade-long project to find and catalogue his collection of ca. 2.700 ammonites according to scientific criteria.

During World War 1, Wetzel fought on the western front. His experiences there significantly influenced his later worldview in which to fight is to survive. In his 1935 publication "Anatomie als Wissenschaft vom Menschen", Wetzel justifies his theses with biological

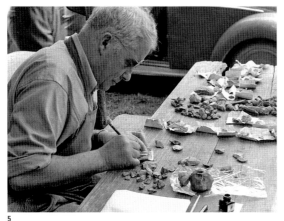

5

arguments: He draws parallels between the behavior and organization of human cells and organs and whole populations. He develops a view of the world, which he summarizes in 1939 with the sentence: "There are at all times battles for Germany, even if no one is shooting!". After the end of the war, Wetzel studied medicine in Heidelberg and in Munich until 1922. Shortly after he began his studies, Wetzel realized that he wanted to continue to work in the field of anatomy. In 1923, he became first assistant at the Institute for Anatomy at the University of Würzburg and completed his habilitation in 1926. In 1936, Wetzel was offered a professorship at the Institute for Anatomy at the University of Tübingen; not just due to his talent for teaching, but also due to his national socialist sympathies, a quality that was a prerequisite for filling positions at the universities since Adolf Hitler seized power. After his appointment, Wetzel turned his attention to university politics. In 1937, Wetzel was made vice rector of the university and became very active in the newly founded National Socialist University Teachers' League (Nationalsozialistischer Deutscher Dozentenbund) – he became their "Führer" in 1938. As "Führer" of the lecturers he was able to make the final decision on all positions to be filled at the university and was instrumental in making sure that the national socialist ideology was well established at the University of Tübingen.

Wetzel was inspired by the spectacular finds Gustav Riek recovered from the Vogelherd cave in the Lone Valley. In 1932, after exploring the area near the Bockstein cave, located further up the Lone River, with some local farmers, Wetzel found evidence for a hidden cave (flint splinters in the sediment dug up by a badger) and began his own excavation near the cave. Wetzel finally received permission for the excavation from the proper agency in Stuttgart after he assured them that he wanted to excavate an area where no one had previously suspected a cave and that he would pay for the excavation out of his own pocket. At the same time, Riek, who had become famous due to his discoveries in the Lone Valley, withdrew from the Lone Valley: He wanted to avoid confrontation with Wetzel because he did not get along with his "character" and preferred to relinquish the field to his competitor. Wetzel did not end up having to pay for the excavation out of his own pocket, his research was financed through the SS "Ahnenerbe" starting in 1935. He wrote adept letters and reports to Reichsführer SS Heinrich Himmler, deftly keeping him fascinated by Wetzler's continuing research in the Lone Valley. Himmler was especially interested in Wetzel's idea of finding new find sites through the tales and stories told by the local population – it brought to mind a parallel to Heinrich Schliemann's work and successes in Troy, a vision that Wetzel was happy to foster in order to secure financial support for his research from Himmler. Wetzel recovered spectacular finds during the campaigns at the Bockstein and the Hohlenstein massif located downriver: A Neanderthal resting place including an inventory of stone tools near the Bockstein cave, a Mesolithic skull burial at the Hohlenstein and, on the last day of excavation in 1939 before the dig was stopped due to the start of the war, the ivory fragments that would, decades later, be assembled to form the well-known Lion Man figurine. Wetzel carried out his excavations using a modern and interdisciplinary approach that was not common at the time, yet the prehistoric experts of the time were hostile towards the archeological outsider and criticized him for it.

After the end of the Second World War, Wetzel was relieved of all his duties and removed from all of his state offices due to his national socialist past. The post-war university concentrated all of its hate onto him as the "evil genius of the university". Although he could be granted the fact the he was a "misguided idealist and not an unmerited fighter against the darkest characters among the Nazi rulers" (decree of the post-war university rector Schneider) he would always be remembered as the "declared representative of a one-sided and obsessed Nazism" at the University of Tübingen. In 1953, Wetzel was able to return to the Lone Valley. Considering his difficulties in Tübingen, the excavations at the Bockstein and the Hohlenstein can also be seen as an escape into a parallel world. Wetzel was well liked by the local population of the Lone Valley. After his early death in 1962, the University of Tübingen showed some leniency. In a letter of condolence sent to his widow, the university states that Wetzel "served the University of Tübingen to the best of his abilities during difficult times and made an effort to preserve it from even worse developments that the trouble times brought with them".

Wetzel reacted by increasing their efforts to initiate SS excavations under the flag of Himmler's "Ahnenerbe": The most famous excavation resulting from these efforts is probably the SS excavation at the Celtic princely burial mound Hohmichele near the Heuneburg on the Upper Danube.

Riek and Wetzel both wanted to remain in Himmler's good graces and made use of his limited understanding of Germanic sacred sites and groves. In 1937, Riek published his first young adult novel with the title "Die Mammutjäger vom Lonetal", in which the bear killers (the Neanderthals) and the mammoth hunters (early modern humans) of the Vogelherd played a central role. He sent Himmler a copy of the book; Himmler in turn felt reminded of David Friedrich Weinland's legendary novel "Rulaman" (1878). Personal difference quickly caused Riek and Wetzel to become enemies rather than friends. After one of the first SS excavations at the Haldenstein cave in 1936, Riek decided to refrain from any future excavations in the Lone region and yielded the (valley) floor to Wetzel. It finally came to a confrontation between the two in 1939 after Riek adopted the opinion of Julius Andree (1898–1942), who heavily criticized Wetzel for sloppy documentation during the Stadel excavation in his book "Der eiszeitliche Mensch in Deutschland und seine Kulturen". Andree was also working under the patronage of the "Ahnenerbe" and later for "Einsatzstab Reichsführer Rosenberg". Wetzel's reaction to these accusations was understandably testy and both archeologists wrote to Himmler, who unsuccessfully tried to attempt reconciliation, each accusing the other of character flaws.

Gustav Riek, director of the Prehistoric Institute at the University at Tübingen since 1935, was conscripted to service in the Waffen SS in 1939. Wetzel continued to work on his political career throughout the war. However, his career came to a surprising end in the summer of 1944 when he resigned from his position as director of the teacher's league and the NSDAP.

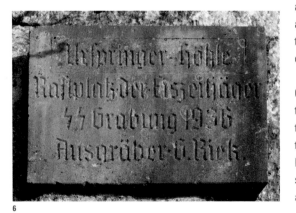

6

In December 1947, Otto Völzing began his first shift in the König
mine in Neunkirchen in the Saarland. His second career began as
an underground mineworker with the Saar mining company and
culminated in his position as director of various mining schools.
Otto Völzing was born in 1910 in Groß-Umstadt in southern Hessia
The discovery of a stone aged tool near his hometown prompted
him to study geology and mathematics at the University of Giessen
and get his PhD in 1937. During his studies, he explored the sur-
roundings of Groß-Umstadt through geological and archeological
excavations under the supervision of the Institute of Geology and
Paleontology and the State Office for the Preservation of Historical
Monuments in Mainz. He was also an assistant in a research
project with a focus on the content of phosphorus in different
types of rocks.

In 1937, Robert Wetzel became aware of the geologist and assigned
him as director of the excavation, which marked the beginning
of systematic exploration of the Stadel cave at the Hohlenstein.
Wetzel was tied up in Tübingen due to his political responsibilities
and was not able to supervise the excavation personally. He was
glad to have found an experienced professional such as the geologist Völzing to take his place. In the first year of excavation, Völzing
reported spectacular finds such as the skeletal remain of a Neanderthal or the Neolithic "bone wreckage site" with numerous human
bones. On the last day of excavation in 1939, it was Völzing and
his workers who recovered the ivory fragments that would, decades
later, be puzzled together to form the Lion Man as we know him
today. After the war, although he had taken up his new position,
Völzing continued to follow news of Robert Wetzel's excavation

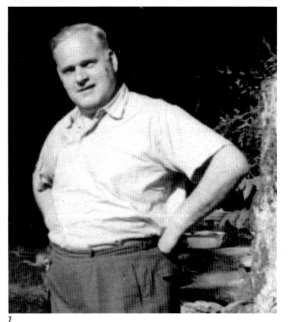

7

in the Lone Valley with great interest. Wetzel made note of the
Völzing's numerous visits to the site with his mining students in his
diary, and Völzing also provided help and advice on the organization
of the challenging excavation at the Bockstein slope. Völzing stayed
in contact with the museum at Ulm up until his death in 2001 and
followed the developing story of the Lion Man and its renewed
reconstruction with great interest. His observations and information, especially about the end of the excavation in 1939, were
valuable clues for the reconstruction of the discovery of the ivory
fragments. Due to reasons of health he was never granted a look
at the reconstruction of the statuette itself.

He had underestimated the resistance from other influential politicians in his
efforts to convert the University of Tübingen to a "Reichsuniversität". Toward
the end of 1944, Wetzel was "punished" and commanded to work on preservation
projects for the "Ahnenerbe" at the Siegfried line. At the same time he signed
up for the "Volkssturm" and carried out target practice in the basement of the
Institute for Anatomy in Tübingen. Wetzel was convinced of the "Endsieg" for
the Germans until the end and continued to proclaim to the leaders of "Ahnenerbe"
up until March of 1945 that he would place the focus of his future archeological
research on the study of race.

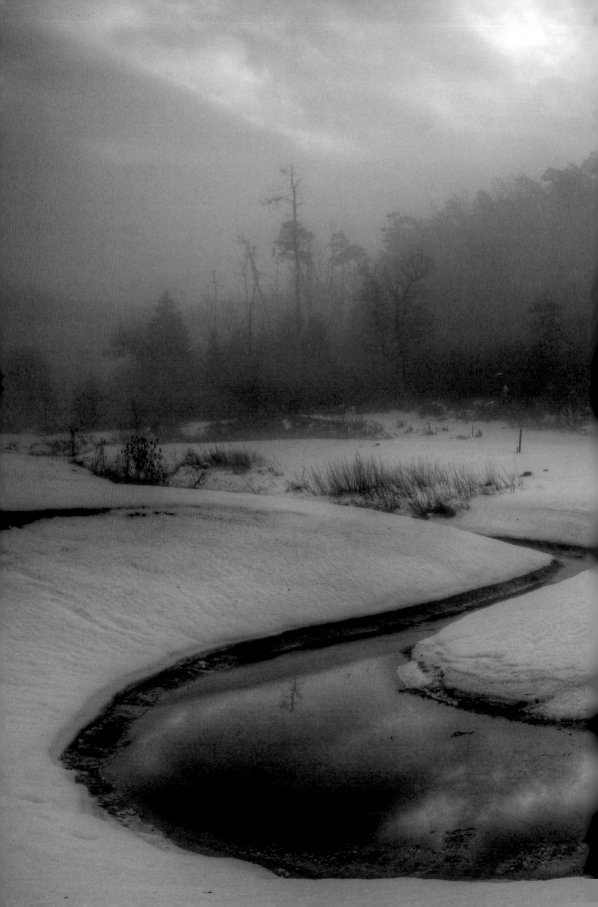

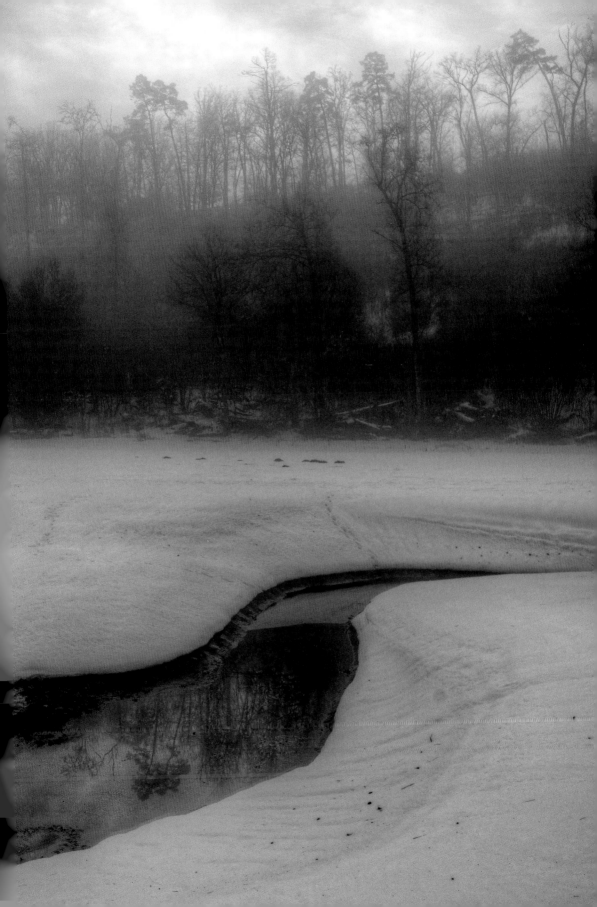

A VERY SPECIAL CAVE

THE STADEL AT THE HOHLENSTEIN

KURT WEHRBERGER

"A subterranean cave in a spooky forest", this is the description from 1834 of a cave in the Hohlenstein rock massif, located between the Paleolithic find sites at the Bockstein and the Vogelherd caves in the lower Lone Valley. The Hohlenstein hosts two caves that are 50 to 60 meters deep today. The entrance to the Bären-höhle is located just two meters above today's valley floor, the imposing entrance to the Stadel cave is located a few meters higher and to the east. The wild charac-ter of the rocky landscape around the Hohlenstein was also emphasized by Johann Herkules Haid's description in his guide "Ulm mit seinem Gebiete" from the late 18th century: "A strange cave, consisting of numerous chambers, some of which can only accessed by crawling on one's knees". The cave is best known as the find site of the Lion Man statuette. However, excavations from the 1930s unearthed a whole series of puzzling finds: The mysterious Lion Man, countless human bones from different eras, tales and reports from historic times – they are all evidence for the special character and the spell of the Stadel cave.

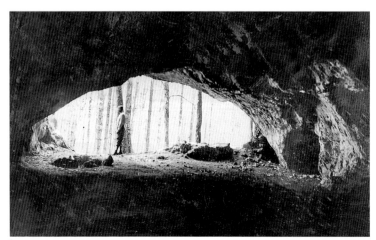

1

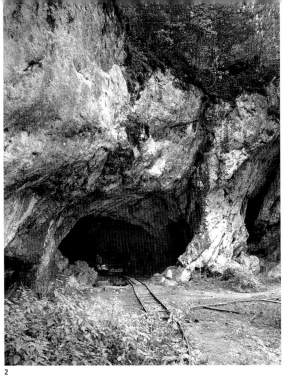

1 The Stadel cave prior to excavations (photo from the summer of 1933). After conclusion of the excavations through Robert Wetzel in 1961, the meter high sediments had been removed in many parts of the cave down to the bedrock
2 The Stadel cave during the excavation in 1960. The sediments were transported out of the cave with a narrow gauge railway, commonly used in mining
3 The Stadel cave 2004

2

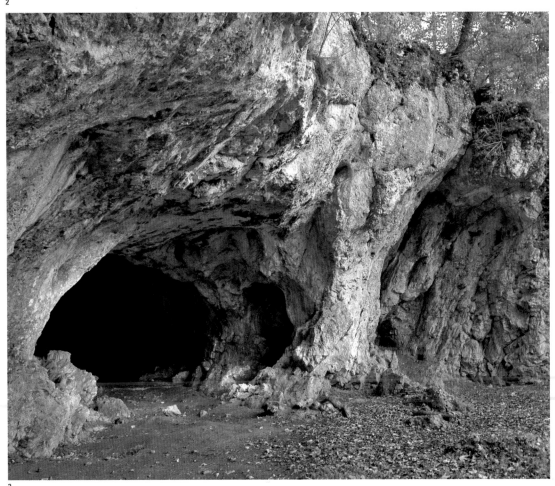

3

4 One of many "devilish" stories from:
K. Keller, Sagen aus dem Lonetal. The
collection was first published in 1986;
the stories were collected orally from
the local population prior to World War 2
5 Sampling of the Neanderthal bone at
the Max Planck-Institute in Leipzig (2008)
6 Hohlenstein-Stadel. Femur shaft from
a Neanderthal, L 25 cm

THE DEVIL FROM THE
11TH CHAMBER

No other cave has been the subject of as many fantastic tales as the Stadel in the Hohlenstein. The devil was said to inhabit the cave – this seems fitting since the deep cave was believed to be an entrance to hell. The hamlet Lindenau, located on the plateau south of the Hohlenstein, also played an important role in the mythology surrounding the cave – the former Lindenau estate included a church and was property of the Bavarian Cistercian Abbey Kaisheim since the early 14th century. It is no wonder that workers regularly unearthed human remains from the cemetery of the church, torn down in 1803. In the tales and stories of the locals, however, these finds were associated with the prehistoric skeletal remains found at the Stadel cave.

The tales also often included geese. Their gaggle was so loud that geese were often used as guard animals in past times. According to legend, if you listen closely you can hear at Lindenau "a goose calling off and on from the Hohlenstein". Geese were even said to have found their way from the Hohlenstein into the cellar vaults under Lindenau.

The special geographic situation at the mouth of the tributary valley that leads from Lindenau north toward the Lone Valley is responsible for the circumstance that sound from the Hohlenstein can be heard at the Lindenau and vice versa. Under certain wind conditions, the rocky slopes and cave opening even reflect and amplify sounds.

"Im Hohlenstein (Stadel) sitzt der Teufel auf einer Goldkiste. Dies ist in der elften Kammer. Die äußere Halle hat Nischen. Die letzte Nische in der großen Halle ist die siebte Kammer. Wer dieses Gold aus der elften Kammer holen will, muß in der siebten Kammer einen Vertrag mit dem Teufel, in dem er sich ihm ganz verschreiben muß, mit seinem eigenen Blut unterzeichnen. Hat er dies gemacht, dann findet er hinten den Teufel auf einer Goldkiste sitzen. Er muß ihm den Schlüssel aus dem Maul nehmen, dann hat er immer Geld genug."

4

Excursus **The Neanderthal from the Hohlenstein**

Johannes Krause, Kurt Wehrberger

At first glance, the human femur (upper leg bone) found in the lower layers near the cave entrance in 1937, does not look particularly impressive. At a second glance, however, certain distinctive features become more apparent: The bone is more massive than in humans today, the attachment site for the gluteal muscles is more pronounced, the shaft is noticeably curved and the cross section is nearly round. All of these features are typical of a Neanderthal

Many decades after its discovery, the bone was again subject of discussion: In 2008, the bone was sampled for the purpose of analysis within the scope of a project to decode the Neanderthal DNA at the Max Planck-Institute for Evolutionary Biology in Leipzig. The bone was again sampled in 2013 at the University of Tübingen. The "Neanderthal genome project" started in 2006 and aims to analyze the Neanderthal genotype using traces of DNA from fossil bones. DNA is isolated, replicated and stored in a so-called sequence library for further analyses. The goal is to successfully sequence the entire genome. Contamination is the most serious threat to this research. It is extremely difficult to separate modern human DNA that may have come in contact with the fossil bone from the fossil DNA. In addition, millennia of bacteria have infiltrated the bone and contaminate the sample with their own genetic material.

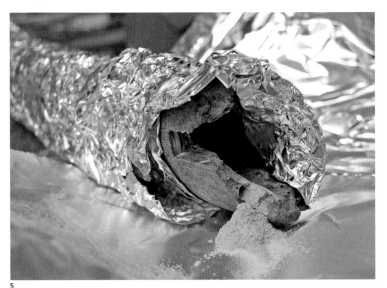

5

For a long time, Neanderthals were viewed as primitive and wild. As research becomes more and more advanced, these perceptions need to change. Today we know that every living non-African carries within them about 2–3 % Neanderthal DNA that was introduced into our genome through mixing about 50,000 years ago, at about the time when our human ancestors

femur. Both epiphyses show signs of biting or chewing and only the 25 cm long shaft of a ca. 160 cm tall individual was preserved. The bite marks clearly show that a hyena dragged it into the cave from wherever the Neanderthal's body was originally deposited. To date, this find from the Stadel cave is the only skeletal evidence of this species of humans in Baden- Württemberg.

left Africa. Research projects like the Neanderthal genome project are working to find out how the evolutionary divergence of modern humans and Neanderthals played out as well as which Neanderthal genes some of us still carry with us today.

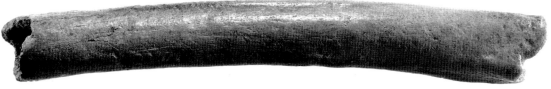

6

7 Excerpt from the council protocol from July 5th, 1591. At the time, the cave belonged to the territory of the imperial city of Ulm **8** Remains of the wall at the eastern portion of the Stadel entrance after the rest was removed in 1937. The tracks from the narrow gauge railway can be seen in the forefront **9, 10** Cut marks on a cervical vertrebra of the woman, seen under the microscope (REM) **11** The head burial at their discovery in July 1937 **12** The ditch with the head burial in the entrance to the Stadel cave (schematic painting 1938)

THE "ULMER MAUER"

During the initial phase of excavations in 1937, Robert Wetzel had the remains of a partially collapsed wall that was blocking the entrance to the Stadel cave removed. Only a small portion of the wall, at parts more than a meter high, was left standing. Today, nothing remains from the so-called "Ulmer Mauer", whose age remained unknown for a long time. "A four foot high rampart wall" was first noted by Oscar Fraas, the first excavator at the Hohlenstein during his explorations at the Bärenhöhle in 1862. He believed that it had Roman origins. Others believed that the wall was build during the Thirty-year war during which the locals used the cave as a shelter. Its true age was not determined until the post World War II period in the 1950s. Enquiries into the Ulm council protocols identified an interesting heading: "Eviction of suspicious persons inhabiting the Hohlenstein". The entry from the late 16th century provided some clues about the age and purpose of the wall.

"Uff meiner gepietenden unnd gunstigen Herrn Herrschafftspfleger bericht den Holen Felsen, Holenstain genannt, anlangendt, darinnen sich viel böser buben und verdechtiger persohnen ufhallten sollen, sollen sie, die Herren, den maurer zu Asselfingen besichtigen lassen, wie und was gestaltt derselbig zu vermauern oder der eingang zu furkommen seye."

7

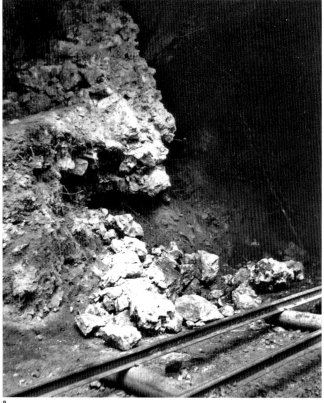

8

Kurt Wehrberger

In July 1937, archeologists found a small ditch with three human skulls located a few centimeters below the foundation of the "Ulmer Mauer". The skulls of two adults and one child – all three facing into the cave – were bedded on the stone pavement and covered with ochre. Anthropological analyses determined that the skulls belonged to a male and a female both aged 20 to 30 and a 2 year old child, possible a family. The head of the child is larger

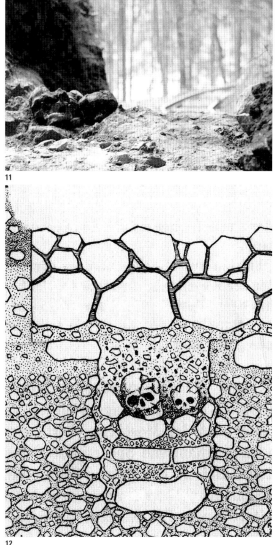

11

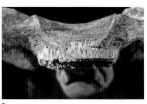

9

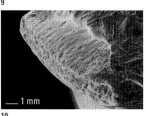

_ 1 mm

10

than is typical for a child of this age and suggests that the child may have suffered from an illness that led to water retention in the brain. Both adult skulls show fractures from an impact with a blunt instrument. The top cervical vertebras were found below the skulls. Cut marks suggest that the heads were cut from the body. Multiple teeth of the perlfish or ladyfish, a ray-finned fish, were found with the female skull. They were probably arranged as a necklace and were placed into the grave as a burial object.

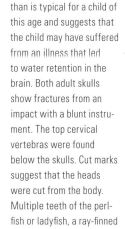

Radiocarbon dating dates the head burial into the 7th millenium B. C., the late Mesolithic. It presents us with a puzzle: Who were the dead and who killed them? What was their relationship to one another? Was it a gruesome ritual, did the murderers bury the heads? Or were they the victims of violence during a war, buried by members of their own group in a way that seems strange based upon our present standards?

12

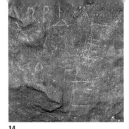

14

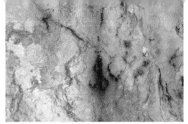

15

THE GRAFFITI

A series of modern graffiti were discovered during the 2008 excavation at the Stadel cave. In addition, inscriptions and symbols made with red or black pigments were found in areas of the cave wall that are not easily accessible today as well as on loose boulders deep inside the cave. Aside from the painted graffiti, carvings and etchings into the cave walls were also identified.

Some of the red inscriptions are located high above the present day surface of the cave floor. They were probably put there by the excavators in the 1930s when the level of the cave floor was a few meters higher than today. The partially washed out inscriptions are difficult to make out but may have been part of the coordinate grid system from the early years of excavation. Deep inside the cave, visitors to the cave immortalized themselves by leaving their name, sometimes even the date of their visit. The cave was better accessible in the past and it was possible to go deeper into the cave than it is today because the passageway is filled with rubble from where the ceiling collapsed into the cave. It is almost impossible to advance further into the cave today. Traces of a lattice from the 1930s at the back of the cave are also visible today in the form of a wooden beam in the cave floor. The iron bar was installed after conclusion of the excavations in the 1960s.

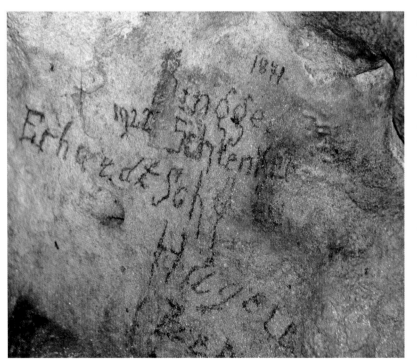

13

Excursus **Cannibals in the Lone Valley?**
Kurt Wehrberger

It is early August in 1937, a few days after the discovery of the buried skulls: Excavators found two pits, lined with stones near the entrance of the cave containing over 1.200 human bones comingled with animal bones, ceramic shards and stone tools from the Neolithic. The bones are heavily fragmented, partially burned and supposedly exhibited cut marks: The excavators spoke about a bone wreckage site ("Knochentrümmerstätte"). The word cannibalism quickly made the rounds. Excavators developed a dramatic scenario based upon the discovery of postholes from a Neolithic palisade underneath the "Ulmer Mauer": A group of people barricaded themselves in the cave. After unsuccessfully defending themselves, they suffered a terrible death.

The sobering resolution to the mystery came in 1995: A detailed analysis of the bone remains with modern methods revealed that the burn marks came from a fire that was lit over the pit the bones were deposited in. The cut marks were only found on animal bones. The human bones include primarily skull fragments, vertebras and long bones. Pelvis, hand and foot bones were missing. The bones came from at least 54 people, males and females alike. About half were from children and juvenile individuals. The composition of

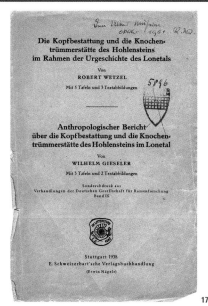

bones shows that the dead must have skeletonized at another location and only selected bones were buried in the cave. Radiocarbon dates confirm the age previously suggested through the shards and stone tools into the late 5th millenium B.C.

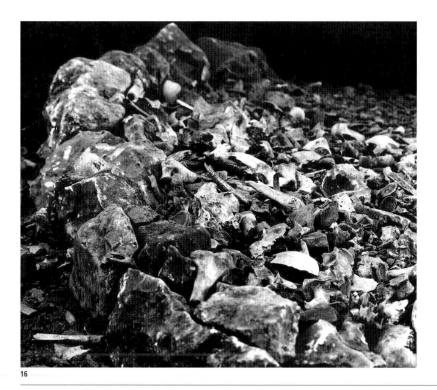

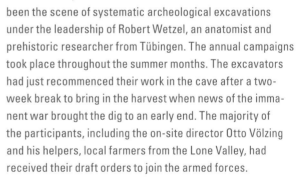

LUCK AND FANCY

THE (ALMOST) NEVER-ENDING STORY OF A DISCOVERY
KURT WEHRBERGER

1939
ON THE SWABIAN JURA NEAR ULM

August 25th: In the Stadel cave in the Lone Valley tools are hastily gathered together, exposed excavation surfaces filled with sediments and the last artifacts packed up for transport. Since 1937, the cave in the Hohlenstein rock massif had

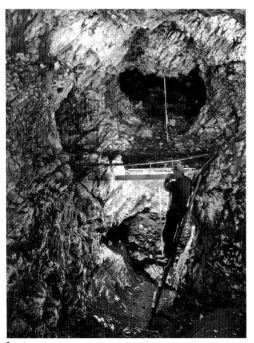

been the scene of systematic archeological excavations under the leadership of Robert Wetzel, an anatomist and prehistoric researcher from Tübingen. The annual campaigns took place throughout the summer months. The excavators had just recommenced their work in the cave after a two-week break to bring in the harvest when news of the imma-nent war brought the dig to an early end. The majority of the participants, including the on-site director Otto Völzing and his helpers, local farmers from the Lone Valley, had received their draft orders to join the armed forces.

The finds from the last days of excavation were brought to Tübingen. The stored objects survived the turmoil of war in the vaults of university without any damage. After the war, additional artifacts from Wetzel's excavations at the

1

Bockstein and Hohlenstein between 1952 and 1961 join the older finds. In 1956, Robert Wetzel had deeded the entire material as a gift to the city of Ulm. After Wetzel's death in 1962, the Museum of Ulm took possession of the hundreds of cigar boxes and cartons full of finds from the Lone Valley excavations.

1969
IN THE DEPOT OF THE MUSEUM

December 8th: For the past few weeks, the archeologist Joachim Hahn has been working in the archives of the museum. His objective: to inventory and identify the finds from the excavations in the Stadel cave. He is currently looking at a box labeled "HS 25.8.39 20. m 6. Hieb". It contains finds from the last day of excavation in 1939 from the 20th meter of excavation from a depth of 100 to 120 cm (one "Hieb" was equivalent to 20 cm of excavation). As he opens the box he notices numerous pieces of worked ivory fragments alongside the animal bones. He shows the pieces to two students who happen to be visiting that day. The three are electrified and feverishly begin to fit the pieces together.

Just a few days later they have pieced together a strange-looking figure – almost 30 cm high, a long-shaped body with two separate legs, the rudiments of a head with the left ear. The upright posture seems human, the head is obviously that of an animal – that of a bear or a lion.

Hahn published his discovery in archeological journals and the daily papers also reported on the impressive find: The title in the weekly journal "Die ZEIT" on March 27th, 1970 reads "The animal-man from Ulm. April fish or sensation?". The newspaper reports quickly spread the fame of "Mugwump" – Hahn's humorous pet name based on a figure out of a novel by the American author William S. Burroughs.

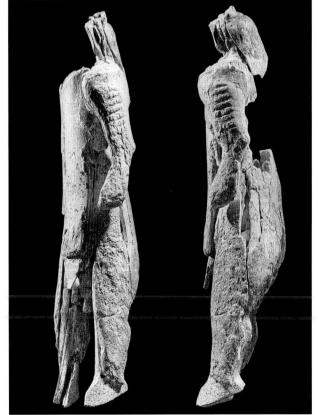

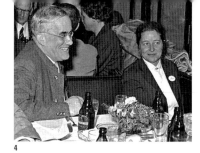

4

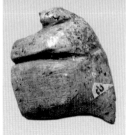

5

1972 TO 1975
MORE FABULOUS DISCOVERIES

December 30th, 1972: A plain cellophane bag without label changes ownership. Its contents: a few pieces of mammoth ivory. Karl Keller, a medicine man from Wiesensteig, who helped Wetzel and Völzing during the excavations at the Hohlenstein as a student, had attended the conference of the Hugo Obermaier-Society in Ulm a few months earlier and listened to the discussion following the presentation of the statuette. He remembered finding and saving some ivory lamellae while cleaning up Robert Wetzel's office at the Institute for Anatomy in Tübingen a few weeks after his death. Otto Völzing and Christa Seewald (1923–2007), director of the Prehistoric collections Ulm (Prähistorische Sammlungen Ulm) – under that name the archeological collections of the Museum in Ulm oper-

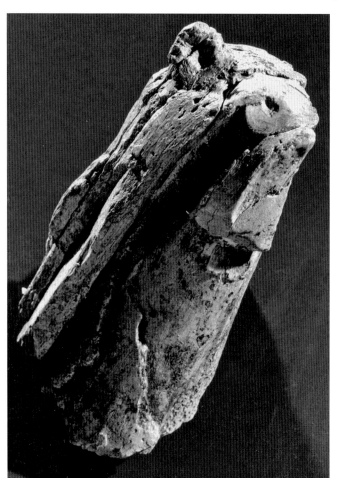

ated as an independent institution from 1970 to 1984 – took custody of these finds. Christa Seewald recognized that the fragments must have been part of the figurine and reported the new findings to Elisabeth Schmid (1912–1994), a paleontologist from Basel, who was working on Robert Wetzel's posthumous publication on the discoveries at the Bocksteinschmiede from the time of the Neanderthals. Schmid had also attended the conference in Ulm and had mentioned her interest in the statuette from the Stadel cave to Seewald. She was later able to match the newly recovered fragments to the statuette.

3

In 1974/1975, a visitor to the museum presented a small box with some artifacts that her son had found while playing in the loose sediments in the Stadel cave. Seewald noticed two pieces of worked ivory and placed them with the other pieces from the statuette. Neither the name of the visitor nor the date when she presented the finds to the museum was recorded. These circumstances and the fact that the back of the cave was secured with an iron bar make this story sound like a fabulous tale.

<u>Excursus</u> **Joachim Hahn und der Löwenmensch**
Johannes Wiedmann

Joachim Hahn was born in 1942 in Chemnitz. In the 1960s he studied at the Universities of Cologne, Bordeaux and Tübingen. He was a specialist for the Upper Paleolithic, particularly for the Aurignacian period. He devoted his doctoral thesis to this time period and it forms the foundation for Aurignacian-based research today. Since 1969, he worked off and on at the University of Tübingen where he received a permanent position in 1973. Finally, in 1988 he was

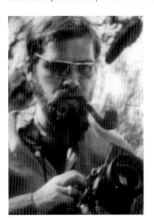

appointed to an extraordinary professorship. In December 1969 he discovered the fragments of the Lion Man in the archives of the Ulmer Museum. He fitted together this animal-man-hybrid with the help of two students, a key moment in his career. Hahn carried out excavations at the Geißenklösterle near Blaubeuren-Weiler from 1974 to 1996, starting in 1977 he also excavated at the Hohle

Fels near Schelklingen. He developed the excavation technique for prehistoric excavations that is still practiced today – the excavated surface is divided into square meters, the square meters into quarters, these are excavated in thin layers and every find is recorded three-dimensionally, the resulting sediments are washed and sieved. During his excavations of the Aurignacian layers at the Geißenklösterle, he found ivory figurines, a tri-color painted stone and the remains of a flute. He published his habilitation, titled "Kraft und Aggression – Die Botschaft der Eiszeitkunst im Aurignacien Süddeutschlands?" in 1986. Its primary focus was on the figurative representations from the Aurignacian period, the oldest know pieces of art to date.

In the 1980s he was instrumental in rebuilding the Prehistoric Museum at Blaubeuren (Urgeschichtliches Museum) together with Hansjürgen Müller-Beck. Joachim Hahn worked (e.g. Banks Island, Canada) and taught (e.g. Ann Arbor, Michigan, USA) worldwide and published multiple research papers and books. He regularly included students in his research and felt strongly connected to them; he always had time or an open door for them. He was also interested in presenting his research to the academic world and also making it available and understandable for the interested public. Unfortunately, Joachim Hahn died in 1997 at the age of 54, much too early for us all

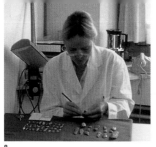

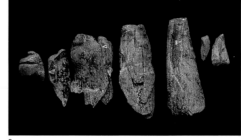

8

9

7 Upper part of the statuette with the temporarily attached fragments to the head (1982)   **8** Ute Wolf during the restoration in her workshop at the Württembergisches Landesmuseum in Stuttgart 1987   **9, 10** During the restoration, the head of the statuette was taken apart and refit with additional pieces – these pictures show the disassembled head together with the newly found fragments during re-assembly   **11** The statuette by the end of the restoration in 1988, H 29.6 cm

1982 TO 1988
GOOD IDEAS AND WRONG TRAILS

<u>1982:</u> It took ten years until Elisabeth Schmid was able to work with the newly discovered fragments. She identified one of the fragments found by the visitor's son in the cave as part of the animal's snout. She was also able to use the lamellae from Wetzel's office to nearly complete the rest of the head. The statuette's head now clearly resembles that of a wild cat.

<u>1983:</u> News that fragments found near the surface of the cave were refit to the figurine were brought to the attention of the State Monumets Office. Eberhard Wagner (1930–1999) decides to excavate at the alleged find site inside the cave – without success, he does not find any additional fragments. More than 25 years later, renewed excavations show that Wagner had not been digging at the correct place.

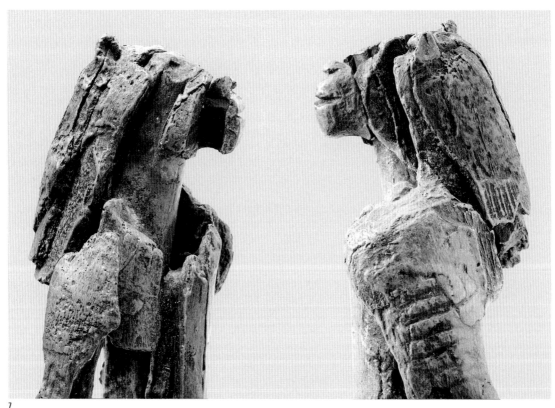

7

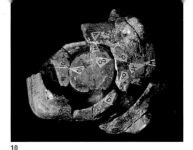
10

<u>1987:</u> Schmid had only attached the lamellar temporarily; the professional restoration of the statuette took place a few years later in the workshop of the Württembergisches Landesmuseum in Stuttgart. The restorator Ute Wolf took on this complicated and difficult task in close cooperation with Elisabeth Schmid.

To begin with, some of the pieces previously glued by Joachim Hahn had to be dissolved; thankfully he had used a soluble glue. Starting from the core piece, the 200 fragments were carefully resorted and refit. About 20 ivory fragments could not be securely fit to the statuette by lack of clear attachments; these were kept separate. During the restoration it became obvious that ivory fragments were missing from inside the figurine as well. These pieces were replaced with a substance made out of bee's wax, artificial wax and chalk, a material that can be easily removed. This mixture was also used to stabilize the core of the body and to reconstruct the assumed shape of the head where ivory pieces were missing. In contrary to Joachim Hahn who had determined the sex of figurine as male, Schmid meant to detect some indices for a female interpretation.

<u>1988:</u> After six months of work, the statuette is returned to the Ulmer Museum. It was possible to refit some additional pieces, but larger portions, primarily of the back and right side of the body, are still missing. They are believed to be lost. This seems to be the end of the adventurous story of the discovery and reconstruction of the ivory statuette, known since 1994 as the Lion Man.

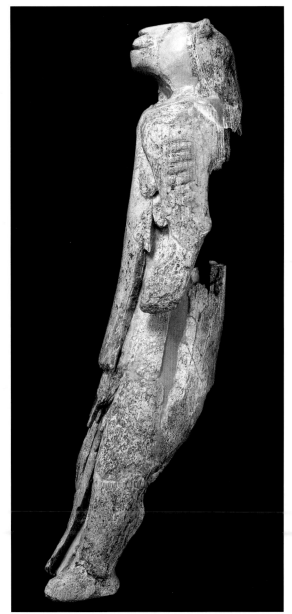

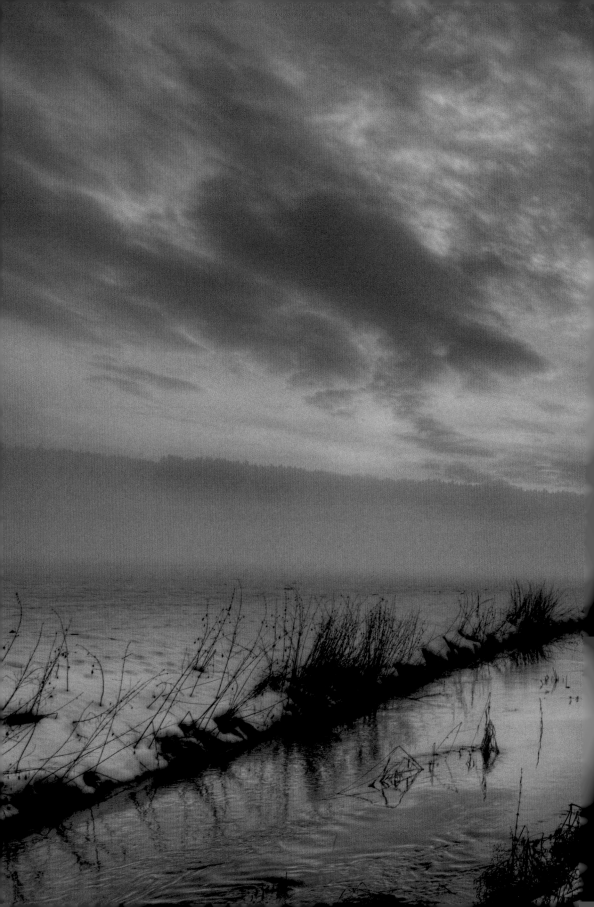

SURPRISE IN THE LOAM

THE REDISCOVERY OF THE LION MAN'S FINDING PLACE AND THE NEW EXCAVATIONS AT THE STADEL CAVE

CLAUS-JOACHIM KIND

In Baden-Württemberg, four caves with archaeological finds are especially important: The caves Geißenklösterle and Hohle Fels in the Ach Valley between Blaubeuren and Schelklingen, and the caves Vogelherd and Hohlenstein-Stadel in the Lone Valley. The so far oldest known pieces of art and musical instruments made by humans were found in these caves' archaeological layers from the begin of the Upper Paleolithic, the so-called Aurignacian period, which dates to 35,000–40,000 years ago. Hence, several government agencies and institutes are working together on an application to have these caves added to the UNESCO World Heritage List.

In preparation for the application, the question was asked what exactly is supposed to be protected through the addition to this list? It quickly became clear that three of the candidates had either been completely excavated (Vogelherd

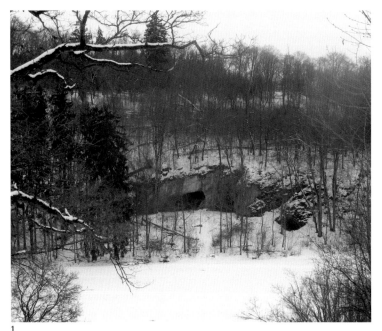

1

cave) or still contained extensive sediments with intact archaeological layers (Hohle Fels, Geißenklösterle). However, not much was known about the Stadel cave in the Hohlenstein, located within the perimeter of the township Asselfingen (Alb-Donau-Kreis). It was assumed that the cave was completely excavated and cleaned out during the excavations carried out by Robert Wetzel between 1936 and 1939 as well as between 1956 and 1961.

To verify the situation, the State Office for the Preservation of Historical Monuments of the Regional Council Stuttgart (Landesamt für Denkmalpflege im Regierungspräsidium Stuttgart) carried out small excavations between 2008 and 2013, at multiple locations inside and in front of the Stadel cave. With these test trenches, excavators attempted to clarify whether archaeological layers remained at the site and how old the possible finds in these layers are. More comprehensive research excavations were not planned. One trench was located in front of the cave, the other about 30 m inside the entrance. The excavations quickly showed that the negative forecasts were wrong. Surprisingly, substantial layers with numerous archaeological finds were recovered at both places.

NEW EXCAVATIONS
ON THE TERRACE IN FRONT OF THE CAVE

Two small exploratory trenches were excavated on the terrace in front of the Stadel cave. One returned very informative results. It was excavated to a depth of 2.5 m without reaching the bedrock and contained a complex sequence of archaeological layers. The older layers contained material that was relocated to the terrace from inside the cave. These layers show more or less heavy influence and transformation due to glacial conditions during their deposition.

The oldest layers from the terrace date to the Middle Paleolithic, the period of Neanderthals in Europe. They are between circa 100,000 and 40,000 years old. Find layers from the Upper Paleolithic, the time period of Homo sapiens, are located above these. The Upper Paleolithic layers can be assigned to different

1 View from the north over the Hohlenstein with the Stadel cave (left), the Kleine Scheuer (middle) and the Bärenhöhle (right)   **2, 3** Hohlenstein. Sieving and inspection of the excavated materials

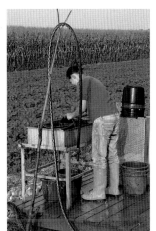

3

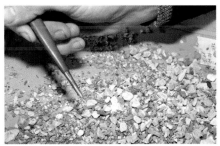

2

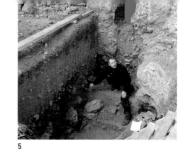

5

cultural periods: These include find sites from the Aurignacian from 40,000 to 35,000 years ago, the Gravettian from about 28,000 years ago, the Magdalenian from about 17,000 to 15,000 years ago and the late Upper Paleolithic from 14,000 to 12,000 years ago. All layers contained typical tools made out of hornstone as well as thousands of animal bones. It was possible to identify numerous different species of animals within the various layers. Cave bear bones were especially frequent in all layers. Some layers contained fauna typical of glacial cold steppes such as reindeer, bison, wild horse, mammoth and wooly rhinoceros. Other layers also included animals that prefer a habitat with trees and bushes such as red deer, wild boar and roe deer. These layers are from a period with more moderate climates during the last Ice Age. Carnivores such as wolves, lynx, cave hyena and cave lions were also represented among the bones.

NEW EXCAVATIONS
INSIDE THE STADEL CAVE

After the excavations on the terrace of the cave proved to be successful, an additional experimental excavation was carried out 30 m inside the Stadel cave entrance. It was located in a small chamber-like opening near the back of the cave after a landing in the shape of a small continuous bedrock ridge. The cave

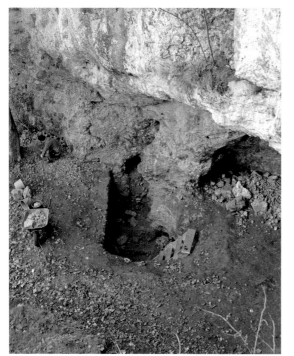

floor rises steeply from this position, which is located about 10 m behind the iron gate installed to secure the entrance to the cave. During work in the eighties of the previous century, excavators believed that they had reached the bedrock and only a thin layer of loam now covered the floor of the cave. Imagine the surprise when the renewed excavations uncovered a complex sequence of layers. The steep slope was artificial and was made up of more or less horizontal archeological, find-rich layers.

4

Laser beams and pixel count –
Documentation at the Hohlenstein
Thomas Beutelspacher

An "excavation" leads to the irreplaceable destruction of a find site through the irrecoverable removal of layers of sediment and any information they may have contained. Therefore, careful and precise documentation has the highest priority in modern excavations. The data gained through rigorous data collection, observation and photos are just as important as the excavated finds themselves.

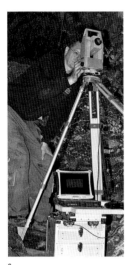

For the documentation of finds and findings at the Hohlenstein, we set up a canvass of survey with a demarcation into square meters. The exact location of all finds and findings were recorded based on the coordinates of this grid, which can, if necessary, be converted to a global set of coordinates (Gauß Krüger or UTM). The vertical height corresponds to the coordinates for average sea level. The most important piece of survey equipment during an excavation is the total station. It consists of an optical tachymeter that is attached to a mobile computer. The tachymeter measures the distance to the object being targeted and records these points three-dimensionally. The object to be measured is first targeted with a laser point by turning and tilting the tachymeter. The devise then measures the distance optically via an infrared beam. The exact position of the target object is then calculated from the two angles and the distance in relation to the previously configured grid. The tachymeter can use this grid to determine its own position as well as the precise coordinates of any object within the grid. The coordinates are then recorded into a database on the computer to compile information about the find layers and to provide an inventory of all measured objects. This survey-database includes all data on the finds and find site and is the basis for all subsequent analyses.

Excavated surfaces, wall profiles and special find contexts are documented with a digital SLR camera (single-lens reflex). Previously measured markers in the sediment make it possible to correct errors due to distortions from the camera lens or less than ideal photographing conditions. In addition, these photogrammetric points can also be used to fit together multiple photos into one single bigger picture on the computer. The points also help to localize the picture in the find site itself. Recently, programs have been developed that allow the user to assemble a three-dimensional image of a site from numerous individual photos (Surface From Motion).

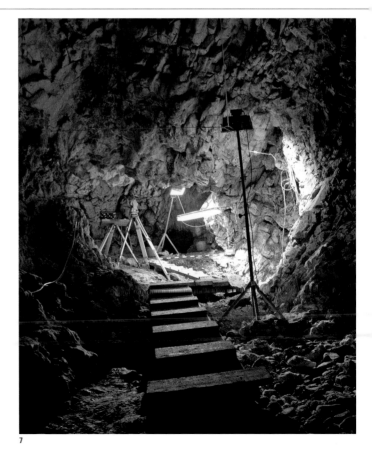

The Lion Man figure was discovered on August 25th, 1939 and was located 1.20 m under the surface in an Aurignacian layer. After its discovery, the excavations were stopped and the finding place was more or less carefully covered with the previously excavated sediments. This is the origin of the steep slope with the artificial incline. The new excavation happened to re-discover exactly the spot where the Lion Man was found in 1939.

Thirteen find horizons were identified during the renewed excavations. The sediments consisted of red, yellow and grey-brown cave loam. The lower archaeological horizons C to M originated in the Middle Paleolithic. Horizon A is made up of three layers and lies directly above the Middle Paleolithic. The ^{14}C dates range between 41,000 and 35,000 years ago and place them into the Aurignacian of the Upper Paleolithic. The position of the Lion Man can be securely identified in this series of layers: He was found in the lower layer of Horizon A and is therefore about 40,000 years old.

The horizons inside the Stadel cave frequently contained archaeological finds. However, direct evidence for the presence of humans in the rear of the cave is rare. Thousands of well-preserved bone and tooth fragments make up the majority of the find material. These include numerous remains from cave bears. There is also evidence for the presence of cave hyenas:

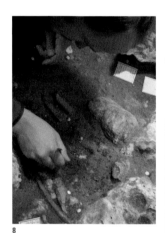

8

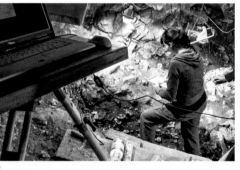

9

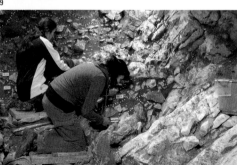

10

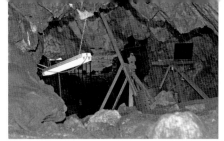

12

This evidence includes bones and teeth from the animals as well as bone fragments from other species that carry very characteristic bite marks from hyenas. The faunal species also include wild horses, reindeer, aurochs, rhinoceros, mammoth and cave lion, among others. The rare human artifacts include stone tools manufactured by Pleistocene humans. The Middle Paleolithic layers include flakes and cores while the artifacts of the Aurignacian are limited to small, flaked chips.

HOHLENSTEIN-STADEL 2013
IDEAL PROFILE

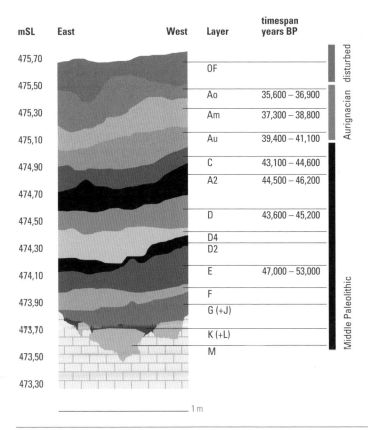

mSL	East	West	Layer	timespan years BP	
475,70			OF		disturbed
475,50			Ao	35,600 – 36,900	Aurignacian
475,30			Am	37,300 – 38,800	
475,10			Au	39,400 – 41,100	
474,90			C	43,100 – 44,600	
			A2	44,500 – 46,200	
474,70					
474,50			D	43,600 – 45,200	
474,30			D4		
			D2		
474,10			E	47,000 – 53,000	Middle Paleolithic
473,90			F		
			G (+J)		
473,70			K (+L)		
473,50			M		
473,30					

_____ 1 m

11

13 Hohlenstein-Stadel. Excavations in 2012   **14** Letter from Robert Wetzel to Hans Schleif dated August 28th, 1939 (Bundesarchiv Berlin Document Center NS 19/1295)

THE EXCAVATED MATERIAL FROM THE 1939 EXCAVATION AND THE LION MAN

To the north of the new excavations with the intact layers lay a small area with a mixture of no longer intact sediments. These are obviously the remains from the 1939 excavation, which were used to refill the previously excavated trench. These previously excavated materials also contained a number of archaeological finds that were overlooked during the original investigation. Bone fragments predominate among these finds. Some stone tools were also recovered. The recovered materials also include hundreds of fragments of mammoth ivory of different sizes. Some fragments show clear signs of being worked and it seemed very possible that they may belong to the Lion Man figurine. Surprisingly, an initial unsystematic attempt to fit the fragments confirmed this. In 2012/2013, the Lion Man was disassembled and then refit as a very complicated three-dimension puzzle. A portion of the new fragments was included in the puzzle. As a result, the Lion Man now looks quite different from the well-known familiar image.

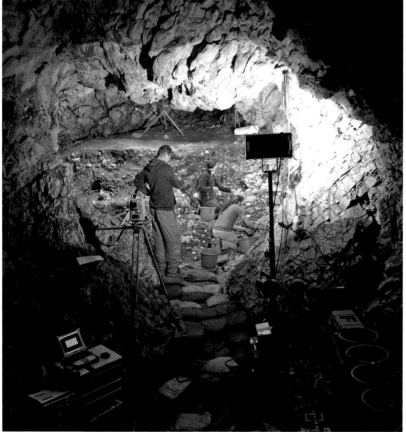

13

"This as final message" –
The events of August 25th, 1939
Kurt Wehrberger

Findings from the recent excavations in combination with known documentation allow us to reconstruct the last hours of excavation at the Stadel cave in 1939: The fragments of the statuette were concentrated within a relatively small area, it had probably partially fallen apart prior to its discovery. It was speculated whether tools,

such as a pick, may have damaged the figurine during the excavation, however the lamellae do not show any serious damages that would support this theory. The fragments were recovered as the excavation was already being closed up. Workers only collected the larger fragments; smaller pieces remained in the ground after the trenches were refilled. Normally the excavated sediments were removed from the cave with lorries. Luckily this was not the case as usual on August 25th, 1939; the excavated sediments with the overlooked ivory fragments remained in the cave.

Barch NS 19/1295

> Wetzel
> Anatomie Tübingen
>
> Tübingen, den 28.August 1939.
>
> SS-Hauptsturmführer Professor Dr.Schleif
>
> Berlin-Dahlem
> Pücklerstr.16.
>
> Lieber Kamerad Schleif!
>
> Falls es Ihnen so geht wie mir, und Sie noch nicht zu besserer Verwendung erfasst sind, mögen Sie hiermit im Nachgang zu meinem Brief vom 22.8. die Vorgänge in Sachen Andree erhalten. Den letzten Brief vom 11.5.39 hat er, wie ich Ihnen schon schrieb, mit allen seinen Zutaten reibungslos eingesteckt.
> Mit herzlichem Dank bestätige ich Ihnen den Eingang der letzten 1000.- RM, deren Absendung für eine optimistische Beurteilung der Weltlage durch das Ahnenerbe spricht. Wir mussten wegen Einberufung der meisten Beteiligten die Grabung abbrechen. Ich bin gestern auf meiner Rückfahrt vom Gebirge, wo ich meinen Urlaub abbrach, noch einmal über die Höhle gefahren. Sie wird gut verschlossen, nachdem sie gerade am allerletzten Tag noch, man kann schon sagen sensationelle Kulturfunde geliefert hat. Nachdem vor allem die jüngeren Kulturen des Magdalénien und Aurignacien, die vorne so gut wie keine Rolle spielten, immer besser geworden waren, je weiter wir nach hinten kamen, sind jetzt beim Anbruch einer zweiten Kammer besonders schöne Sachen herausgekommen. Insbesondere lieferte das Magdalénien eine handlange Knochennadel, zwei durchbohrte, recht anständig erhaltene Anhänger aus Holz !!!! und Bruchstücke einer Elfenbeinplastik. Was sie darstellen sollte, ist nicht erkennbar; die gewollte Schnitzerei ist einwandfrei sicher.
> Dies als vorläufig letzte Nachricht vom Lonetal - Sie sehen, es wird sich lohnen, in ruhigeren Zeiten weiter zu machen. Sollten Sie wider Erwarten den Reichsführer noch einmal sehen, so machen Sie ihm bitte die Freude und sagen Sie es ihm.
>
> Ich selber bin in der unangenehmen Zwitterlage, dass die Sanität ausgerechnet jetzt vor einigen Wochen mich entdeckte und mich aus meiner Einordnung als Infanteriegeschütz-Offizier herauszuangeln versucht. Ausgerechnet jetzt sitze ich zwischen zwei Stühlen.
> Heil Hitler!
> Ihr

We are puzzled by a letter, sent by Robert Wetzel three days after the end of the excavation in the Stadel cave to Hans Schleif (1902–1945), archeologist and architect for the SS research organization "Ahnenerbe" in Berlin. In the letter from August 28th, 1939, Wetzel reported on sensational finds from the last day of excavation, among them the fragments of an ivory figure: "It is not clear what it is supposed to represent, but the carvings are clearly intentional". At the close of the letter, he asks Schleif to inform the Reichsführer SS Heinrich Himmler about the discovery: "This as final message from the Lone Valley for the time being".

This document was only identified a few years ago and provides evidence that Wetzel was aware of the ivory sculpture but refrained from ever mentioning it in any of his publications or journals. Only Otto Völzing mentions "fragments of carved ivory" in an article from 1941. The additional fragments, recovered from Wetzel's study after his death, prove that he had access to at least some of the fragments from the statuette. Why did he not devote himself to these fragments after the war and why did he not continue his research at the finding place from August 1939? The answer to these questions remain a secret, which he took with him to the grave.

A GIANT PUZZLE

RESTORATION OF THE STATUETTE 2012/13

NICOLE EBINGER-RIST
SIBYLLE WOLF

1 The puzzle pieces   **2** Position of the figure in the mammoth tusk

The surprising discovery of numerous additional fragments during the new excavations – carried out by the State Office for the Preservation of Historical Monuments – inside the Stadel cave from 2009 to 2012, set the stage for a renewed restoration of the Lion Man figurine. The statuette had remained unchanged since its last restoration at the Württembergisches Landesmuseum in Stuttgart in 1987/1988. The new restoration took place in the workshop of the State Office in Esslingen. We were confident that the recovered pieces could help complete the fragmentary statue. Surprisingly, it immediately became clear that some of the newly discovered pieces complemented some of the loose fragments from the older excavations and together they could be refit to the Lion Man. They are key finds that allow us to comprehend and appreciate the Lion Man figure in its entirety.

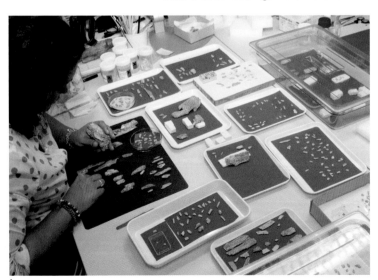

1

POSITION OF THE FIGURE IN THE TUSK
AND PRESERVATION

The restoration process allowed us to gain new insights into the material used to fashion the Lion Man. The ivory for the statue either came from the right tusk of a 12 to 15 year old mammoth bull or from the tooth of an adult mammoth cow whose teeth were fully developed and straight. The head of the figurine is oriented toward the tip of the tusk. The position of the legs is predetermined due to the pulp cavity, the tip of the pulp cavity ends in the crotch of the figure. The outer edge of the arms is made up of the outer tooth cement layer of the tusk. The outer surface of the upper back is also made out of tooth cement. This shows that the circumference of the tusk barely decreases from the feet to the head of the statuette and that the whole tusk was used to carve the Lion Man figure. However, wherever possible, the outer cement layer was removed, making room for the much more attractive dentin surface. Therefore the Lion Man figurine is almost entirely made from the massive tooth dentin. A small hole in the crotch represents the nerve-channel that continues through the figure and out through the head.

Ivory is made up of 60% dentin, 30% collagen and 10% water. The millennia long burial in the ground caused the ivory figurine to decompose; the collagen, which is responsible for keeping the tooth intact, was washed out and disintegrated. The tooth became dry and brittle. The statue first fell apart along the natural growth lines of the tooth. Different processes in the cave sediments continue to influence the state of preservation of the figure: E.g. the outer surface is cracked and eroded primarily due to the influence of water. The surface of numerous other pieces is marked with black patches from the mineral manganese.

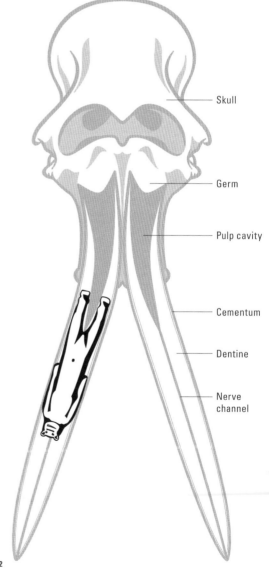

Skull

Germ

Pulp cavity

Cementum

Dentine

Nerve channel

In total, 758 ivory fragments were waiting to be reassembled at the beginning of the refitting process; fragments from the original excavation in 1939 that were not fit to the original statuette and fragments from the excavations in 2009 to 2012. All fragments were analyzed to ensure that they were actually fragments of ivory. 139 fragments were identified microscopically as antler or bone and consequently were excluded from the puzzle.

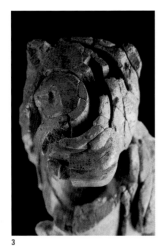

FIRST FITTINGS AND
THE RESTORATION 1987/1988

When Joachim Hahn first reconstructed the figure he was able to assemble 200 of the 260 fragments into a 28.1 cm tall figurine. According to Hahn, the lamellar structure of the ivory suggests that a significant portion of the original outer surface must have flaked off over the years. The body and the legs were reconstructed first; the left leg was almost complete while the right leg and foot were missing some pieces. The exact position of the fragment with the belly button could not be reconstructed exactly. The slightly bent left arm and hand was also completely preserved. In Hahn's description from 1971, he mentions that the cone shaped core of the head and the left outer portion of the head and an ear were also reconstructed and attached; however, these fragments were attached with a degree of uncertainty.

3

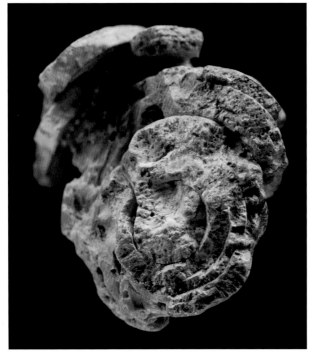

A professional restoration followed in 1987/ 1988 after Elisabeth Schmid had previously temporarily attached some of the newly found fragments in the area of the head. The conservator Ute Wolf from the Württembergisches Landesmuseum in Stuttgart carried out the renewed restoration in the fall of 1987 and the spring of 1988. In 1982, during Schmid's work on the figurine, it quickly became apparent that although she and Hahn had reconstructed a good portion of the fragments, the attachment and gluing had not been very professional or exact. Some pieces were not attached perfectly. Therefore some unattached pieces that clearly belong to the figurine could not be refit.

4

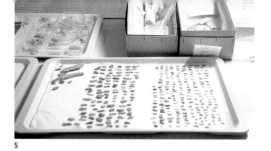

5

That is why it was necessary to dissolve some of the attachments in order to realign the pieces and include the previously unattached pieces. In the course of the conservation, the figure was also stabilized and generally restored.

Wolf disassembled the figure into a number of larger pieces by dissolving the glue at the attachment sites. This was not easily done because Hahn and Schmid had used conventional glue (UHU). When she realized that individual fragments as well as the larger assembled pieces were extremely fragile, Wolf decided to impregnate individual pieces with cellulose nitrate to conserve them. She labeled 58 fragments that she planned to attach to the figurine with consecutive numbers; eight of them could be attached to the figure. Additional pieces were also assembled into four larger fragments, however these could not be attached to the Lion Man. Wolf used the same glue as her predecessors. The figure was still missing some pieces after the renewed assembly. Because the head was the most incomplete, Wolf decided to reconstruct the missing pieces using a mixture made from wax and chalk that could easily be removed again if additional pieces turned up at a later time. This mixture was used to reconstruct visibly areas that were missing pieces as well as to stabilize the figurine from the inside out. After the restoration process, the Lion Man had gained stability and a new and improved appearance. The statuette was now 29.6 cm tall.

VIRTUAL RECONSTRUCTION AND
THE RESTORATION 2012/2013

Numerous new ivory fragments from the most recent excavations were thought to belong to the Lion Man figurine and first unsystematic attempts to match these pieces to the statuette in the fall of 2010 were promising. At the time, the original figurine was not available for comprehensive restoration work, therefore the pieces were scanned three dimensionally using X-ray computer tomography. The advantages for the Lion Man and the ivory fragments from the older and the new excavations are that the reconstructed portions made out of the wax-chalk mixture can be hidden and the old glued bonds can be removed virtually. By doing this, it was possible to virtually disassemble the Lion Man into individual pieces on the screen. The new pieces could now be fit to the figure without actually having to take it apart. Three of the scanned new pieces ended up serving as key pieces to attach two additional pieces from the older collection onto the back of the figure. After this successful reconstruction attempt using X-ray computer tomography, the figure itself was presented to the State Office for the Preservation of Historical Monuments in 2012 for restoration and conservation. The primary

6 Preserved original surface in the area of the head   **7, 8** Dissolution of the wax-chalk reconstructions as well as the glued bonds and impregnation with cellulose nitrate from the old restorations   **9** Numerous lamellae of different sizes in the pulp cavity on the back of the figure. The nerve channel is visible in the crotch of the figure

goal was to complete the three dimensional puzzle by attaching the identified pieces from the older and the new excavation to the actual Lion Man figure. The Lion Man was about to undergo the most comprehensive reconstruction and changes since its original discovery: The characteristic appearance of the figurine, which had been presented to the public for the past twenty-five years, has been changed significantly through the most recent restoration.

In the head and leg regions, pieces were fitted to the correct part of the figure but not to the exact position in the tooth – individual layers of the tooth were missing. Formerly, pieces were glued on a layer or two below the correct position. Initial analyses of the original figure quickly made clear that one of the biggest challenges was how to best dissolve and remove the old glue attachments without damaging the ivory so that the Lion Man could be disassembled into its individual parts. From the point of view of a conservator, it was necessary to remove the old glue because it was starting to negatively affect the material of the statuette –

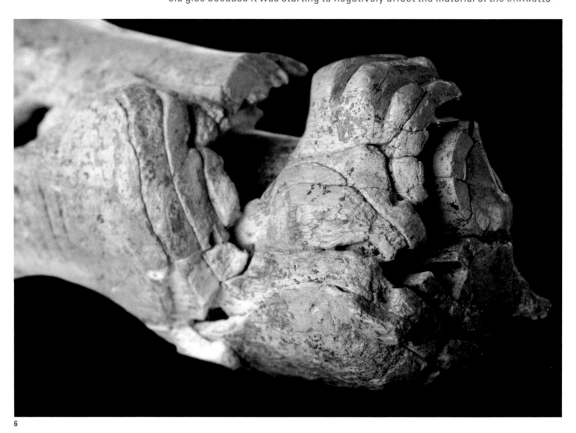

6

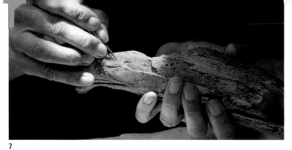
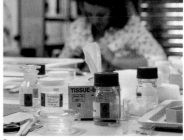

7

8

the glue had hardened over the years and was now harder than the ivory itself. While dissolving the glue and taking the statue apart piece by piece, more glued bonds than had been anticipated were uncovered, the old bonds had been covered up by the wax-chalk additions to disguise the yellowing bonds. All wax-chalk additions were also removed and the Lion Man was completely disassembled into its individual pieces. All of the pieces were now included in the big puzzle. The old pieces were reassembled together with the pieces from the new excavations.

The individual fragments are tinged different colors and heavily eroded depending on their position in the tusk and in the figurine as well as due to their immersion in the sediments and the conditions of their discovery. It is, at best, possible to differentiate between the three main layers, tooth cement, dentin and the original worked surface of the figurine. The surface is yellowish-brown and highly polished. However, e.g. the back of the statuette was exposed to weathering and the surface is heavily eroded, therefore its appearance varies significantly. This made it

difficult to correctly identify and assemble pieces that belong together. The identification of the inner pieces (dentin) was complicated by the circumstance that these pieces could only be identified based on the curvature of the ivory, a result of the concentric growth of the tooth. However, this was only possible for the larger, better preserved pieces. By taking close look at the lower third of the statuette it was possible to count 28 fallen apart layers of varying thickness. It proved to be nearly impossible to assign individual pieces of dentin to one specific layer.

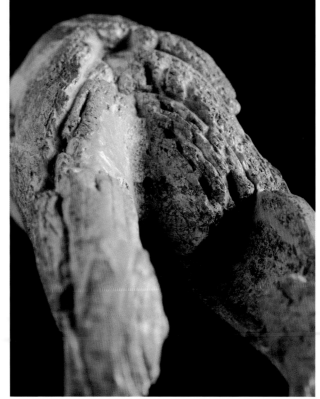

After the statuette had been taken apart, the surfaces and edges of the fragments became visible. It some instances it was problematic to find neighboring pieces that fit since the edges were broken and rounded due to their immersion in the ground and the prior reconstruction attempts. The color of the fragments is also only partially helpful in finding matching pieces because we were often able to place a light piece directly adjacent to a darker piece.

9

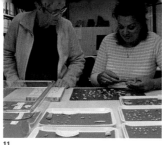
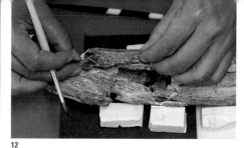

11

12

The relatively small number of fresh broken edges proved that fewer pieces than we assumed were broken recently. These fresh edges are characteristically white and sharp. Pieces with clear traces of having been carved and polished were especially lucky because they could be easily correlated to each other. This was the case for the left ear, the right half of the snout and a part of the face that carried a characteristic notch. While working with the over 600 ivory fragments, it quickly became clear that not all of the pieces belonged to the Lion Man. Their texture and their coloring did not match that of the figurine.

In a final step of the puzzle, the fragments of the figurine were all assembled together. The greatest difficulty was that intermediate layers were missing within the figurine. Therefore it was not possible to place all pieces in their exact position. These gaps were filled with ridges made out of microcrystalline wax, which is unobtrusive but very stable. We decided to use this wax because it is very functional and also because it does not irreversibly damage the material to which it is attached. In general, the mammoth ivory is warped due to the millennia-long immersion in the cave sediments. This means that it was not always possible to find an exact or perfect fit. A right mammoth tusk was used to initially create the statue; this tusk naturally curves toward the inside and to the left. This has to be taken into consideration in the course of the reconstruction. The reconstruction tried the patience of all of the participating restorators – besides the two authors,

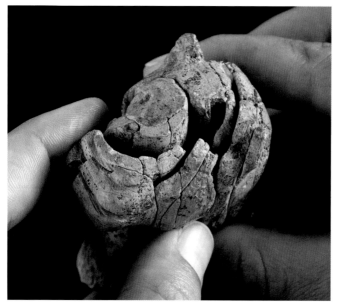

Anette Lerch from the State Office for the Preservation of Historical Monuments – because there was not guarantee for success as an incentive and required a great deal of perseverance.

10

BONDING, COMPLETION
AND RECONSTRUCTION

From a conservator's point of view, although the ivory in the figurine is relatively dry, it is not necessary to carry out any additional conservational measures such as impregnating the material. The reason for this is that ivory is a hygroscopic material and is always in equilibrium with its environment. As a result, the moisture content of the ivory is balanced with the relative humidity of the air around it. Therefore it would be damaging to apply any substances to the statuette because they would inhibit this permanent exchange. As soon as ivory is glued or a foreign material is added to it there is a strain on the material. The previous impregnation of the material could not be reversed, but it was possible to reduce the levels; this significantly reduced the symptoms of yellowing on the surface. The current bonds were made with a reversible and non-aging acrylic resin. We decided against the reconstruction of missing pieces based solely on aesthetic reasons so that the general impression would not be falsified. The missing pieces do not negatively impact the overall appearance of the Lion Man, in fact, the lamellar structure of the material, which has become more pronounced due to the figure's deposition in the sediment, is now put on display as well. Therefore, the authenticity of the figurine has been preserved. The attachment of the right arm to the figurine is a reconstruction because only individual ivory fragments from the arm were preserved and it was not possible to define the exact attachment site.

10 Missing pieces in the sequence of layers in the area of the head **11** The restoration labor: The two conservators Anette Lerch (left) and Nicole Ebinger-Rist (right) **12** Fitting the large arm lamellae from the right side **13** Loose fragments with rounded edges from the old restorations

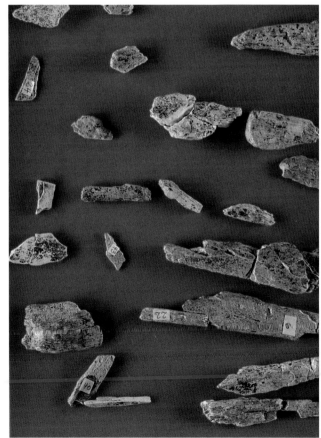

13

14 Completion of the left shoulder
15 Back view of the Lion Man before (a) and after the restoration (b)

THE REWARD
LION MAN 2013

The 2012/2013 task of restoring the Lion Man was successful in spite of the complex ivory material and its specific characteristics. It was possible to fit many pieces from the older collection as well as many newly discovered pieces from the most recent excavations. The circumference of the head increased. The right portion of the snout was completed. We also found and attached the original surface of the right ear. Attaching the left shoulder blade made it possible to actually see the intersection of the arm and body for the first time, thereby strengthening the animalistic impression of the figure. The missing portion of the back was found and filled the so far largest hole in the statuette. The figure is now 31.1 cm tall. The lamellae, previously identified as a piece of the right chest area in 1989, were confirmed due to new insights into the figurine. The inner portion of the statue was filled with fitted pieces of dentine. A staff made out of Plexiglas previously held this portion of the statue, the junction between the upper and lower body, together. Today, this area is stabilized with the recovered original materials. Significant changes to the structure of the right leg were also made due to additional layers of ivory. Numerous small pieces of ivory were added all over the statue. They do not make a big difference on their own, however, they complete the statue, e.g. a small piece of the original surface in the area of the left upper leg. These pieces close small gaps and serve as connecting pieces for larger fragments. In sum, they make a significant contribution to the overall form on the Lion Man sculpture. The proportions of the figure have changed in length as well as in circumference.

The story of the discovery and the restoration of the Lion Man is very complex. We have applied modern and time-consuming methods of restoration to complete the appearance of the Lion Man as far as possible. The intense examination of the material mammoth ivory and the shape and form of the fascinating Lion Man allowed insights into the design and creation process of the

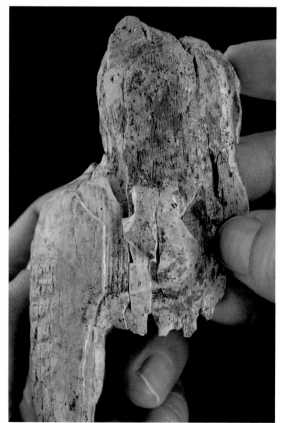

14

ice-aged artist. It became apparent that the restoration process contributed significantly to the preservation of the figure. The new attachments, such as the left shoulder, shed light on new aspects of the figurine and allow us to gain new insights that aid us in the interpretation of the famous Lion Man. Seventy-four years after its discovery, its history and the intention behind its creation remain fascinating.

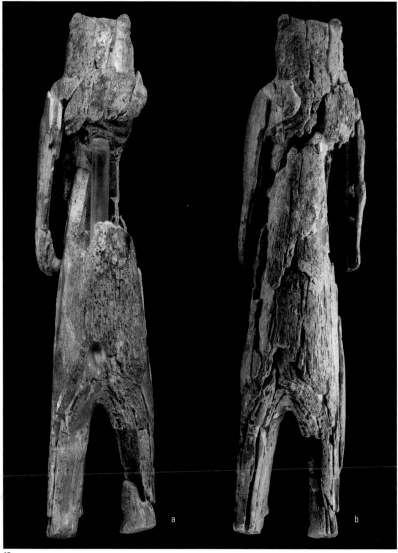

a   b

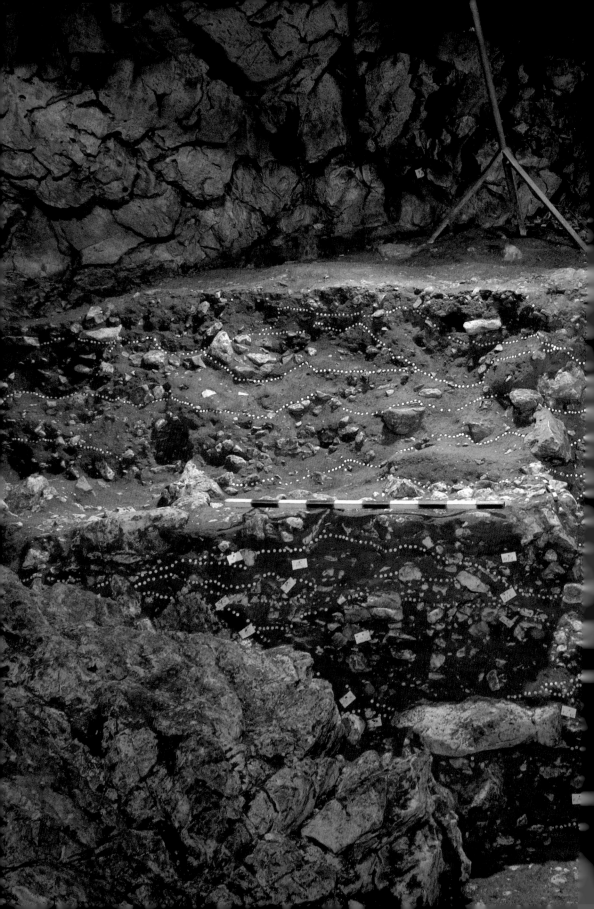

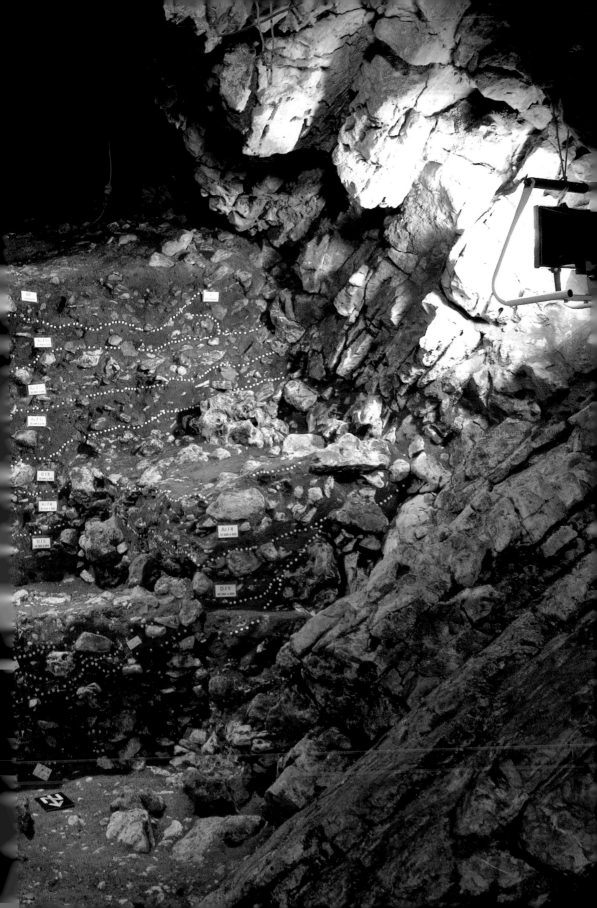

FROM HEAD TO TOE

A CLOSER LOOK AT THE LION MAN

NICOLE EBINGER-RIST
CLAUS-JOACHIM KIND
KURT WEHRBERGER
SIBYLLE WOLF

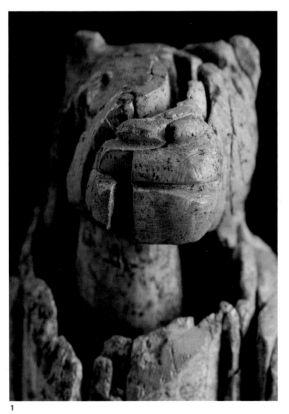

1

The Lion Man figure had fallen apart into hundreds of individual pieces during its millennia-long burial in the cave sediments. After the successful restoration of the fragments from 1939 excavation and the pieces from the renewed excavation from 2009 to 2012, the statuette is now much more complete than it was after the previous restoration in 1987/88. More than two-thirds of the original material has been restored and the Lion Man's appearance has been significantly altered. It became clear that the figure was carved from the right tusk of a young mammoth or an adult mammoth cow that curved naturally towards the left. The figure was worked as straight as possible. The artist attempted to compensate the natural curve of the tusk so that the Lion Man is presented in an upright posture. As a result, the orientation of the statuette varies slightly from the natural orientation of the tusk.

CHEST, STOMACH AND BACK

During the restoration process it was possible to refit and complete a significant portion of the long back. However, the original surface of the stomach and the back was only partially preserved. The upper portion of the body is also missing significant pieces from the inner core. Due to the short neck, the transition from the chest to the head is relatively abrupt. The chest bulges forward but does not have any gender-specific characteristics. The original surface of the front of the body was only preserved in the vicinity of the bellybutton. The bellybutton was worked similar to the eyes through a scraping and curving motion and is nearly circular. The groin area is emphasized through deep notches; the crotch is clearly

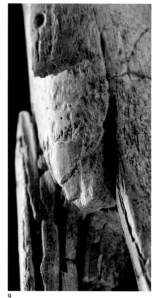

9

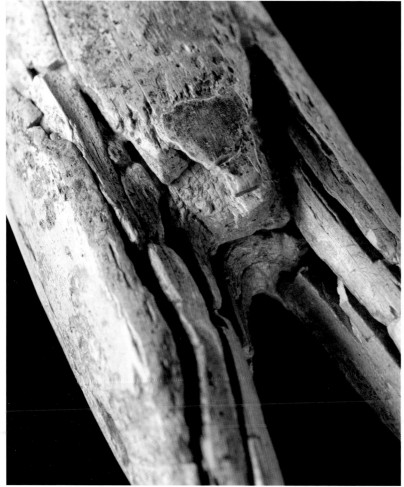

8

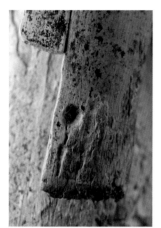

10

defined. A three dimensional, triangular platelet was carved from all sides and attached to the pubic region. Its surface seems highly polished, similarly to the other pieces with a preserved surface. This platelet is interpreted as stylized male genitalia.

LEGS AND FEET

The buttocks were not explicitly formed and the back continues directly to the upper thighs. The shape of the thighs and the calves of both legs are clearly human. The right knee was shaped with great care and the hollows of both knees are represented on both sides. The left ankle is also clearly defined while the right ankle is not completely preserved; therefore it seems weaker. It looks as though the figure is standing on its toes. The toes are slightly angular and carving marks are visible on the sole of the left foot.

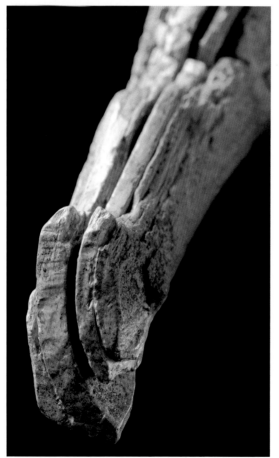

11

INTERPRETATION

Although many details are visible and it was possible to complete the figurine significantly, it is clear that there are still some pieces missing. This pertains primarily to pieces from the inside of the figure and the original surface. It is not possible to explain conclusively what has happened to these missing pieces.

The statuette is a curious mixture of two creatures. The head is that of a big cat, probably a cave lion. This is most clearly expressed by the snout and ears. The long upper body, the forelegs and the shoulder also fit this interpretation. However, the bellybutton, the legs with their clearly defined knees and ankles and the upright posture of the creature are clearly human. The renewed restoration has strengthened the characteristics of a lion. The general proportions, e.g. the long upper body and the relatively short legs, also support the impression of a non-human creature. Nevertheless, the human characteristics are also quite clear and detailed. Therefore, the initial interpretation of the figure from the Hohlenstein-Stadel as an animal-human hybrid – a Lion Man – persists after the renewed restoration process.

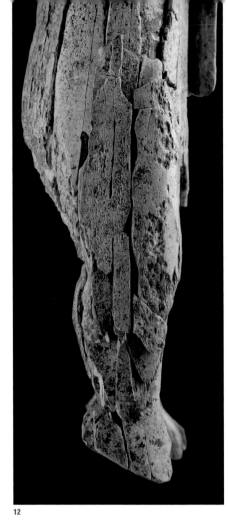

12

Many details of the figure, such as the head, shoulder, elbows, knees and heels, were carved to look very natural. Other elements, such as the paws, the pelvis and the feet are stylized. The sex of the figure is a recurring question. After contrary interpretations in the past the carefully worked genital now allows to identify the figurine as a male one. Its general proportions also speak for the male gender.

The left and right side of the Lion Man were worked differently. Only the left side of the figure was decorated with notches on the ear and arm, the latter could be interpreted as tattoos. The right side of the body seems rougher than the left side. This is most obvious in the right arm. It is possible that the artist first worked on the right side of the statuette and perfected his technique while working on the left side. The back and the front side of the figurine were not worked smoothly; instead they were worked in gradual steps towards the legs. This could be a design element that is supposed to represent fur on the back and stomach of a big cat. It could also be interpreted to represent a disguised human who is wearing a lion skull and pelt.

The artist who created the Lion Man must have obviously been a very detailed observer with good crafting skills and artistic capabilities in order to be able to reproduce something that he or she had observed in real life out of a piece of mammoth ivory. However, a creature like the Lion Man does not exist in real life. Therefore the figure is also evidence for the power of the imagination of the people from the Paleolithic, just a few centuries after Homo sapiens migrated into Europe.

10 Bellybutton   **11** Tool marks on the sole of the left foot   **12** Right leg with the thigh, knee, the hollow of the knee, calve and slanted foot

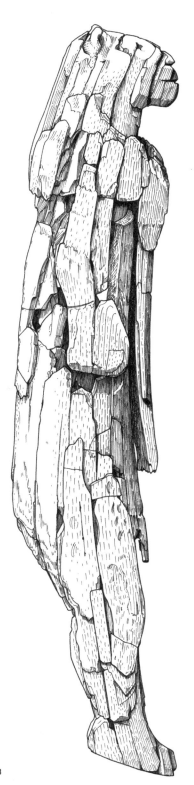
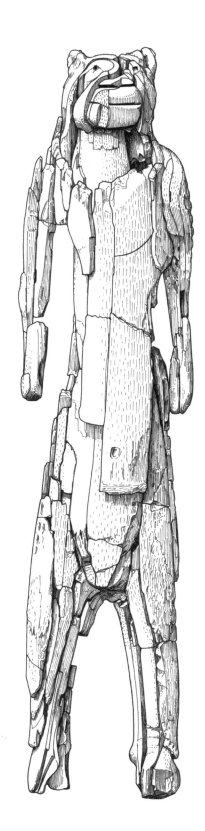

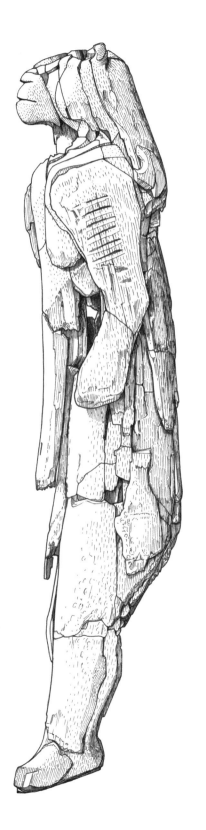
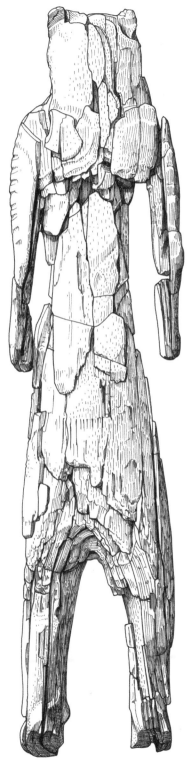

13 Drawing of the statuette from the front, back and sides, H 31.1 cm

ON THE MOVE

THE DISPERSAL OF MODERN HUMANS
MICHAEL BOLUS

The Lion Man from the Hohlenstein-Stadel was found in a layer that dates to the beginning of the Upper Paleolithic, the Aurignacien, which is more than 40,000 years old. Human skeletal remains are very rare from the Aurignacian period and the fossils that have been found all belonged to anatomically modern humans, not to Neanderthals who inhabited Europe and lived parallel to modern humans for a number of millennia. Therefore it is safe to assume that modern humans created the Aurignacian.

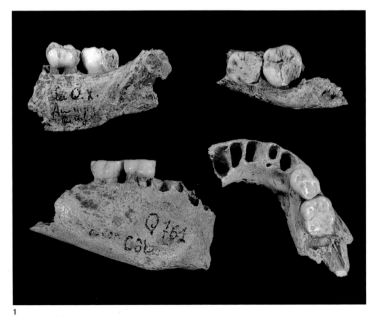

1

MODERN HUMANS ON THE MOVE

Anatomically modern humans first evolved in Africa. The earliest specimens were found in Ethiopia and are nearly 200,000 years old. The first modern human bones that were found outside of Africa are only about 100,000 years old and come from the region of what is now Israel. More than 50,000 years later, modern humans first stepped onto the European continent.

The oldest evidence for modern humans in Europe is quite new: The recently discovered two teeth from the Cavallo cave in Italy are probably 45,000 years old. The teeth were not recovered from an Aurignacian layer but from the Ulluzzian layers, a culture from the transition period between the Middle and Upper Paleolithic. The finds from the Peştera cu Oase cave in Romania are slightly younger, about 40,000 years old and were found without any archeological contexts. Once they reached the European continent, modern humans quickly spread out all over as evidenced by the 42,000 year old maxilla from Kent's cavern in England; the archeological context is also unclear at this site. The oldest human remains from a clear Aurignacian context are the 38,000 year old jawbones and teeth from the French find site La Quina-Aval.

1 Jaw fragments with teeth from anatomically modern humans from the French site La Quina-Aval   **2** Skull of an anatomically modern human from Peştera cu Oase cave in Romania

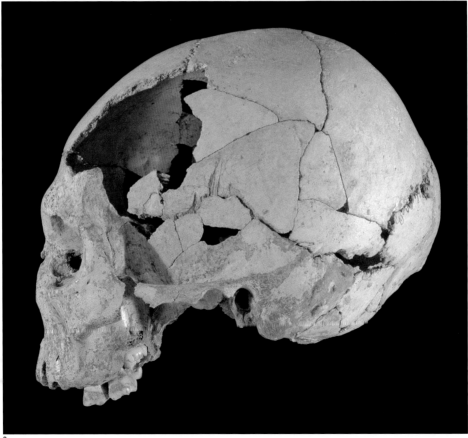

A NEW CULTURE
IN EUROPE

Although the fossil record is quite scarce for the early phase of modern humans in Europe, the cultural legacy of these humans is enlightening evidence for their presence and dispersal. The Aurignacian, between 43,000 and 27,000 years before present, plays a prominent part in this expansion. Find sites from this period are know from the Iberian Peninsula, from Western and Central Europe with branches in Great Britain, from Southern and Southwestern Europe as well as from Eastern Europe at least as far as the river Don. Though there are regional differences and foci, the Aurignacian is the first complex of the Paleolithic that is prevalent throughout most of Europe. Similar finds existed in the Near East as well as parts of Central Asia. The Protoaurignacian, also archaic Aurignacian or Fumanian, is similar yet distinguishable from the Aurignacian and occurs in the northern Mediterranean area, Northern Spain and into Southern France and Italy. The Aurignacian gave rise to numerous innovations that did not exist, or at the least only in their early stage, during the time of the Neanderthals. For example, stone working is characterized through the production of blades and bladelets and many other new types of tools appear. Typical for the period are carinated- and nose-end scrapers as well as carinated and busked burins that were probably used as cores for the production of slim bladelets. The tool inventory also includes simple blade scrapers, different types of burins, pointed blades, blades with heavy edge and truncation retouch and splintered pieces.

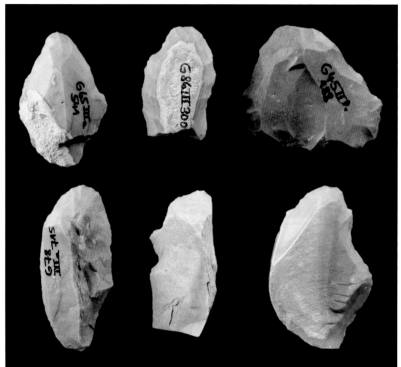

Tools made out of organic materials, bone, antler or ivory, play a similarly significant role in the tool inventory. Bone points with a split base are especially characteristic for the early phase of the Aurignacian. They occur in numerous caves
of the Swabian Jura, however, not in the Hohlenstein-Stadel. Bone points with a
massive base are frequent, too. Polishing tools and awls are more frequent while
other tool types are more rare. Finally, characteristic of a definitive Aurignacian
are figurative art, personal ornaments and music.

It stands to reason that the expansion of the Aurignacian in Europe can be correlated with the dispersal of anatomically modern humans in the region. In fact, the
Aurignacian seems to be an European phenomenon and numerous innovations
in the material culture, and possibly also various social developments, can trace
their origins back to this period. The oldest evidence comes from the Swabian
Jura and it seems significant that 40,000 years ago, this region is already host to
the entire Aurignacian "package" of innovations, including pieces of art, jewelry
and musical instruments, that is more rare or not at all present at other Aurignacian find sites. It is logical that modern humans dispersed from the Near East or
Central Asia, travelling along the Danube through Southeastern Europe and eastern Central Europe, without having the entire Aurignacian package at their disposal. The Swabian Jura then served as a centre of innovation in which the Aurignacian was developed and finally passed on. However, the development of the
Aurignacian was on no account unilateral or monocentric as demonstrated by the
Protoaurignacian / Fumanian in
Northern Italy and Northeastern
Spain. It is probable that modern
humans dispersed along at least
one other main route along the
northern Mediterranean coast and
through various addition centers
of innovation.

3 40,000 year old carinated- and nose-
end scrapers from the Aurignacian of the
Geißenklösterle cave in the Ach Valley
4 Plate from a publication by Édouard
Lartet (1861) displaying typical finds from
his excavation at Aurignac in Southern
France. The site gave its name to the
Aurignacian. The plate includes representations of bone points with a split base,
polishing tools, awls, as well as pointed
blades all made out of flint   **5** Bone
points from the Aurignacian of the Vogelherd cave in the Lone Valley

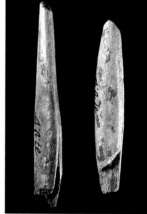

5

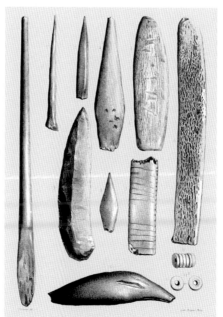

4

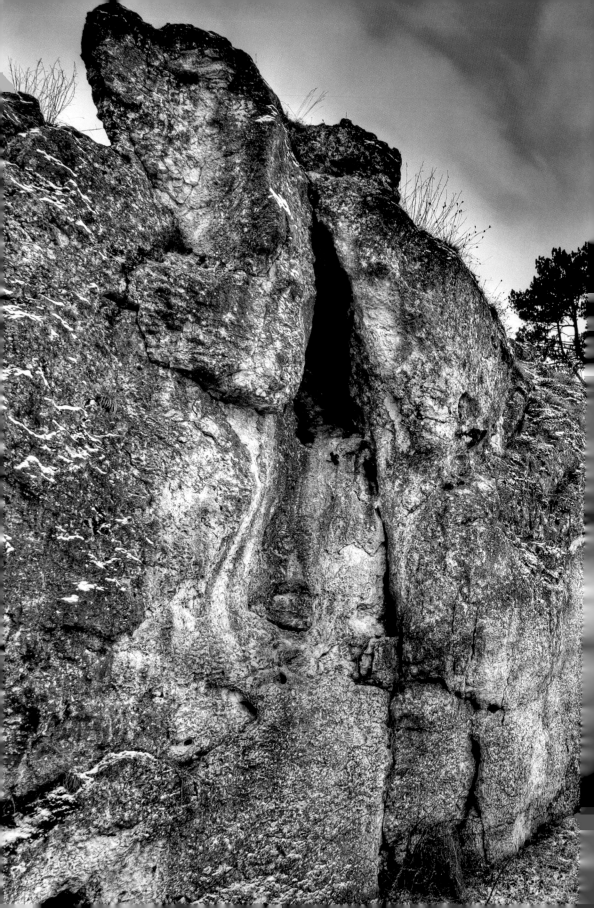

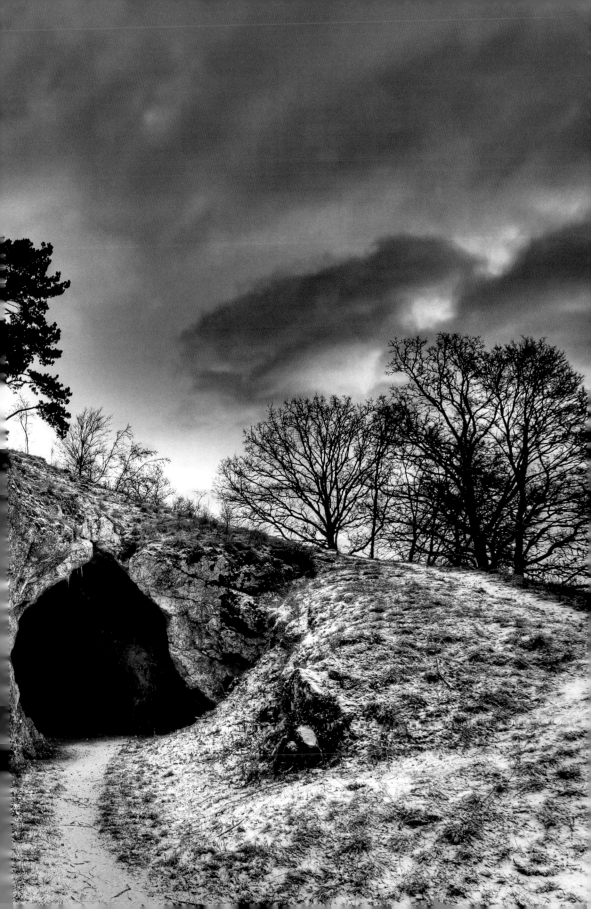

THE VOGELHERD HORSE AND THE IVORY FIGURINES FROM THE SWABIAN JURA

AN ESSAY ON THE WORLD'S OLDEST PIECES OF ART

HARALD FLOSS

Sometimes it is necessary to remind myself not to take for granted the fact that I am surrounded by the oldest pieces of art known and made by mankind. The State Premier of Baden Württemberg Winfried Kretschmann recently visited the University of Tübingen and I was honored to be among those asked to introduce him to the activities of our alma mater. We debated back and forth on how best to use the few available minutes to exemplify that 40,000 years ago, the rough and lonely Swabian Jura was the birthplace of human cultural history. In the end, the beauty of the Vogelherd horse captivated Mr. Kretschmann without the need for accompanying words. Sometimes, our fantastic finds simply speak for themselves.

OLDEST ART?

It is necessary that we critically question this assertion again and again. Are the ivory figurines from the Stadel, the Vogelherd, the Geißenklösterle and the Hohle Fels really the world's oldest pieces of art? Note, based on our current knowledge, the figurines from the Jura are quite simply the oldest sufficiently dated pieces of figurative art in the world! However, surprisingly, international discourse presents different opinions on this and I would like to explain why. On the one hand, there exists a general competition to find the "most beautiful" or "most significant" and in archeology, to find the "oldest". For a long time, other continents were not explored as thoroughly as Europe. Also, early hominids prior to Homo sapiens were often discredited so that it was inevitable that someone would attempt to save e.g. the Neanderthal's honor. Another argument states that early evidence of human culture was not preserved very well and that it is necessary to specifically search for these remains. There is also a certain skepticism that art and music can have developed and spread so quickly without a precursor. And finally, many

1 Vogelherd. Horse figurine, ivory, L 4.8 cm

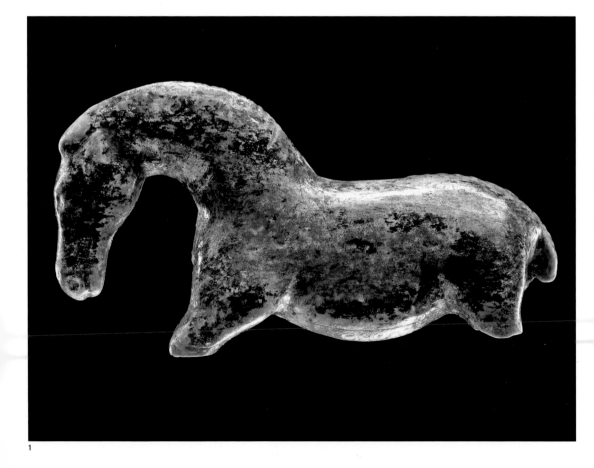

1

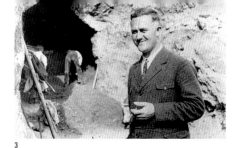

3

researchers are driven by an exaggerated political correctness, trying to eliminate Eurocentric research by travelling to the most remote corners of the earth in order to try their luck there. Historically, Germany plays a prominent role in this argumentation. As a result, it wasn't until the 1980s – fifty years from their discovery – that French research acknowledged the Vogelherd figurines for what they are.

In sum, in the past decades, the discussed premises have resulted in a downright run to find pieces of art that are older than those of the Swabian Aurignacian. In fact, some artifacts were found, primarily in Africa, that attest to a sense of aesthetics in early Homo sapiens. These include early jewelry as well as pieces of ochre and eggshells with geometric designs. Also, new evidence presents astounding insights into the Neanderthal's sense of aesthetics; For example, they are attributed with the use of pigments and feathers as well as the construction

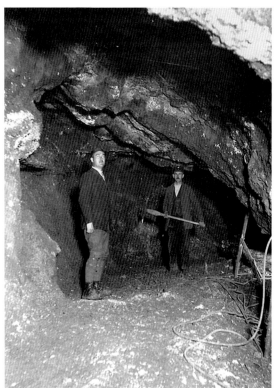

and arrangement of graves. Nevertheless, we are still waiting for evidence of cultural artifacts from somewhere in the world that can match, in age and complexity, the phenomenon of the Ice Age art, either from the caves or in the form of objects, which we find in Europe 40,000 years ago.

2

WHY EUROPE?

What was apparently so special about our small Europe, an appendix of Asia?
During a recent trip to Japan, I had a light bulb moment. Anatomically modern
humans arrived in that region at around the same time during which they expanded
into Europe. Yet ice-aged art, whether cave art or mobile art, does not exist in
Japan. The cognitive capabilities of Japanese Homo sapiens were identical to
those of their the European counterparts. However, the former probably settled in
an uninhabited landscape while Homo sapiens in Europe encountered Neanderthals. We believe that this possible meeting and its consequences are the primary
factors that distinguish Europe from all other continents. The climatic conditions
40,000 years ago were not dramatically different from those during other phases
of the last Ice Age and other regions of the world. And the cognitive capabilities
of modern humans of the Aurignacian were also not significantly different from
those of modern humans from other time periods or geographic regions. Therefore,
the cognitive approach is no longer valid as an explanation for the oldest art. It
is nothing more than "ambient noise", since we are in fact humans and not flies.
Trying to consider the cognitive abilities of humans as a catalyst for the creation
of art and symbolism is like trying to explain the phenomenon Bayern München
through the existence of grass and leather. In our opinion, the explanation for the
beginnings of art and music are to be found in the realms of demography. The term
so-called cultural modernity has led us to a dead end. The creation of the Grotte
Chauvet or the Lion Man from the Stadel cave have nothing in common with the
creation of a regularly formed stone tool by a Neanderthal 100,000 years ago or
the activities of a Homo sapiens who fashions a blade or eats mollusks for dinner
during the same time period in Africa. We are confident that the social conditions
in the European Middle and Upper Paleolithic were quite different. This is not
meant to judge one or the other. Quite the contrary: Those authors who are
continuously trying to show that Neanderthals are our equals have determined
that we are the measure of all things, not the authors who dare to emphasize
the differences.

THE IVORY FIGURINES FROM THE SWABIAN JURA
QUESTIONS AND ANSWERS

But now, on to the actual topic of this paper: We have decided on a concise question-and-answer mode in order to outline the most important facets of the Aurignacian art from the Swabian Jura.

*How many find sites on the Swabian Jura contained pieces of art from
the Aurignacian?*
Four: Hohlenstein-Stadel and Vogelherd (both from the Lone Valley),
Geißenklösterle and Hohle Fels (both from the Ach Valley).

How many figurines were found?
About fifty, including some fragments. It is not yet clear whether the recovered fragments belong to different figures or to one and the same. By far the most objects were recovered from the Vogelherd cave.

What material are the figurines made out of?
Primarily out of ivory. One mammoth relief from the Vogelherd is made out of bone, another questionable piece from the same find site was worked from sandstone.

Who made these figurines?
Anatomically modern humans made them. The human remains found at sites associated with Aurignacian artifacts are always Homo sapiens. Neanderthal remains were never found together with Aurignacian artifacts.

Which individual within the group made these figurines?
We can't know that exactly. The individual figurines are very characteristic, which suggests that they belonged to different people. However, it is possible that specialists who were especially talented (or chosen?) created the figurines.

How old are the figurines?
Radiocarbon dates and the stratigraphic evidence suggest that the oldest figurines are over 40,000 years old; the youngest are about 30,000 years old. The finds from the material previously excavated by Gustav Riek could also be assigned to the Aurignacian. Analysis of the jewelry, through Sibylle Wolf, has shown that the forms typical of the Gravettian period were only found in the Ach Valley and are not present in the Vogelherd.

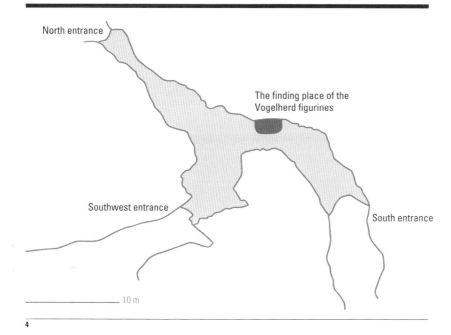

North entrance

The finding place of the
Vogelherd figurines

Southwest entrance

South entrance

10 m

Why is the Swabian Jura so important within the context of cultural history?
Anatomically modern humans migrated into Europe 40,000 year ago. They followed
rivers such as the Danube and used them as landmarks. The Jura presented them
with caves, raw materials for stone knapping and hunting fauna, thereby furthering
their Paleolithic success story.

*Is it true that the art from the Swabian Jura first appears during the developed
Aurignacian?*
No! The dates from the Geißenklösterle and the stratigraphic position of the Venus
from the Hohle Fels are evidence that Aurignacian art on the Jura existed at the
start of the Aurignacian period.

Are there any Middle Paleolithic precursors to the Aurignacian art of the Jura?
No.

Is Joachim Hahn's theory of strength and agression correct?
Yes and no. It is true that dangerous animals such as lions, mammoths and
rhinoceroses play a special role among the figurines. However, new finds from
the Vogelherd and Hohle Fels include smaller and inconspicuous animals such
as porcupines, birds and fish.

5 Rock face with the Geißenklösterle cave in the Ach Valley near Blaubeuren-Weiler

6 Selection of small figurines from the Aurignacian period from the caves of the Swabian Jura:
a–c Mammoth and mammoth fragments
d Mammoth mid-relief
e Anthropomorphic figurine
f Fragment (miniature Lion Man)
g Mid-relief of humanoid figurine ("Orant")
a–c, e–g ivory, d bone, L max. 6.9 cm (a–e Vogelherd, f Hohle Fels, g Geißenklösterle)

What is so special about the ivory figurines from the Swabian Jura?
Their mobility (with the exception of the Lion Man); they can be worn as ornaments (eyelets); they are all individual and unique; they are tactile hand charmers (polished surfaces); the symbols on their surface.

Are there any other find sites with Aurignacian art in Europe?
Yes, more and more. For a long time, the structuralistic approach to defining Paleolithic art by A. Leroi-Gourhan 'forbid' a classification of developed and aesthetic pieces of art into the beginning periods of the development of art in the early Aurignacian. The discovery and dating of the cave paintings in the Grotte Chauvet and other discoveries changed this. We now know of numerous pieces of art from the Aurignacian period, e.g. from Romania (Coliboaia), from Italy (Grotta di Fumane), from Austria (Stratzing), from Belgium (Trou Magrite), from the Swabian Jura, from Burgundy (Arcy-sur-Cure), from Southwestern France (Chauvet, La Baume Latrone, Aldène), from the Dordogne (Castanet, Blanchard, La Ferrassie, Cellier etc.) and from Northern Spain.

Are there any comparable successors in the Upper Paleolithic?
Yes, there are numerous animal and humanoid figurines especially from the Gravettian in Lower Austria and Moravia. These finds associate the Aurignacian with the developed Upper Paleolithic. The Venus from the Hohle Fels is the archetype of all female figurines that occur in the Gravettian.

How long did it take to make the figurines?
Through experimental archeology we know that it took more than a day to make one of these figurines.

Where were the figurines made?
The large amount of ivory debris at the Vogelherd and the Hohle Fels suggest that the figures were created on site. At the Stadel cave, it is possible that the Lion Man was created and then brought into the cave once it was finished.

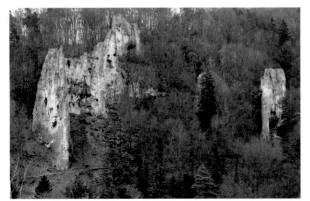

5

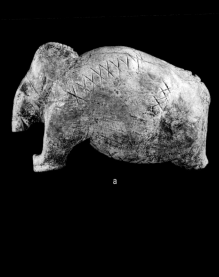

a

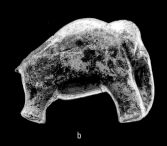

b

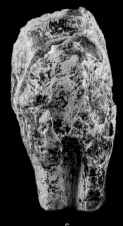

c

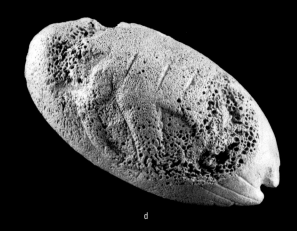

d

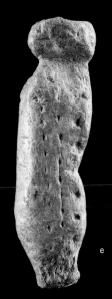

e

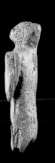

f

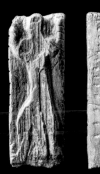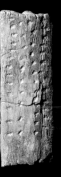

g

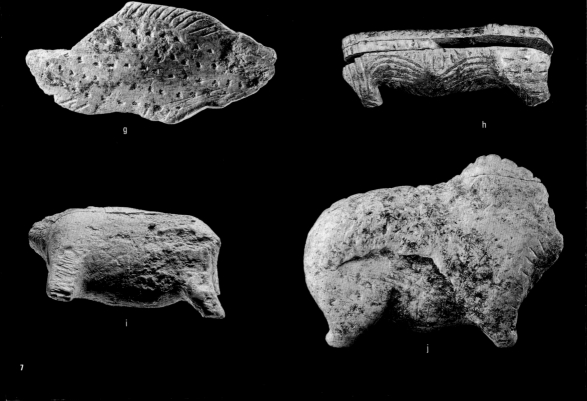

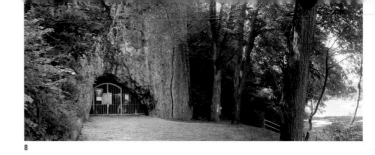

8

7 Selection of small figurines from the Aurignacian period from the caves of the Swabian Jura:

a–c Lions
d Water bird
e Head of a horse
f, h, i Fragments of figurines
g Fish
j Bison
ivory, L max. 7.2 cm
(a–c, f–j Vogelherd,
d, e Hohle Fels)

8 Entrance to the Hohle Fels cave near Schelklingen

What was the purpose of the figurines?

The most difficult question is asked at the end. The archeological context of the figurines in the find sites and within the individual layers is difficult to reconstruct due to the, in part, older excavations (Vogelherd). In the Geißenklösterle, the ivory figurines were found among the common settlement remains. In the Stadel, the Lion Man was found in a niche toward the back of the cave where the common settlement debris became more rare. The findings in the Hohle Fels are very interesting. The so-called Venus was found in the immediate vicinity of the flute made from a vulture bone. It is not impossible to imagine that these two objects were used within the same (ritual) context. The finds themselves also convey a very clear message. We believe it is inappropriate to trivialize the meaning of the statues by implying that they were simple child's toys. The Lion Man from the Stadel and (the miniature version) from the Hohle Fels, the orant from the Geißenklösterle and the very feminine Venus from the Hohle Fels are clearly evidence of a more profound phenomenon. The figurines speak a very clear symbolic language. Hunter-gatherer communities are often animistic. These figurines may be the home of their ancestors. The composite beings bear witness to these interactions with the ever after. The creation of these figurines required a high expenditure of energy. It is possible that they were part of rituals that served to ward off evil spirits. After all, it was well known that the animals that were killed during the hunt might have been host to spirits. This gave rise to a problem that could only be solved through rituals. The exaggerated sexual characteristics of the Venus from the Hohle Fels may also point in this direction since it also has so-called apotropaic traits. In many archaic societies, the exaggerated display of sexual parts is used as defensive magic. These actions are called pubic or breast lore. Hopefully future excavations at the Swabian Jura will recover further evidence that will help solve the archeological puzzle of the meaning of the ivory figurines from the Swabian Jura.

NOT JUST PRETTY

JEWELRY FROM THE BEGIN OF THE UPPER PALEOLITHIC
SIBYLLE WOLF

The cave sites Hohle Fels, Geißenklösterle and Sirgenstein in the Ach Valley as well as the Vogelherd, Hohlenstein-Stadel and Bockstein-Törle in the Lone Valley on the Swabian Jura contained numerous extraordinary Aurignacian-aged pieces of jewelry. They are very variable and characteristic for the region. Almost all pieces were fashioned out of mammoth ivory. These pieces are the first evidence

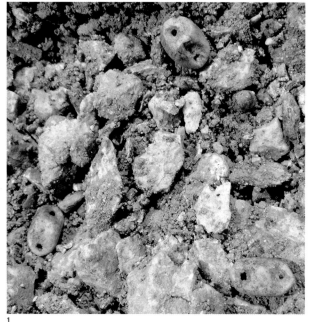

for three-dimensional forms carved out of the raw material ivory in the history of mankind. In 1870/71 Oscar Fraas found perforated animal teeth at the Hohle Fels near Schelklingen. Since 1987, excavations took place annually in the tunnel and alcove in front of the large hall and 217 pieces of jewelry made out of ivory and from all stages of the production process were found. The beads are an average of one centimeter in size and were frequently recovered during the sieving and sorting of the sediments. The beads were found in all five Aurignacian layers (AH) IId to Vb and date uncalibrated to between 29,500 and 35,700 years before present. AH IV contained 87 pieces, the most of all the layers. The most frequent type of bead is the double perforated bead. It dominates the jewelry inventory and constitutes half of all known beads. The find inventory of the Hohle Fels also includes

1

numerous unique pieces that cannot be assigned to a specific group of forms and that express the artist's or the wearer's desire for individuality. Other forms include the single perforated bead, the knob-shaped bead, the figure eight-shaped, the basket-shaped, the disk-shaped and the ring-shaped bead. Another special form is the double perforated bead with a wedged-shaped projection, a modification of the frequently formed double perforated bead. Interestingly,

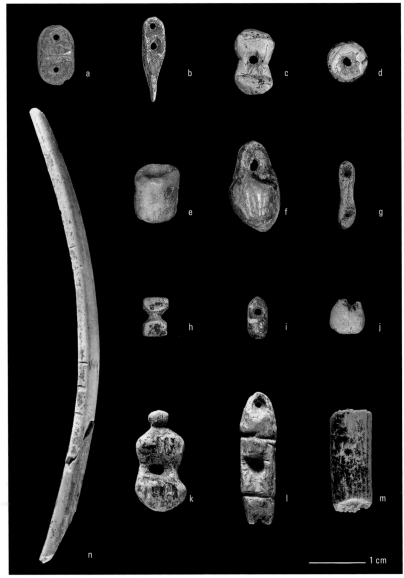

1 cm

3 Vogelherd, mammoth made out of
mammoth ivory, discovered in 1931

4 Pendants and beads, Aurignacian
a–c pendant and double
     perforated bead
d   single perforated bead
e   double perforated beads
f, g single perforated beads
h   basket-shaped bead
i   double perforated bead
(a–d Geißenklösterle, e–h Hohle Fels,
i Sirgenstein), all made out of mammoth
ivory

the basket-shaped bead and the knob-shaped bead were only found in the younger
layers IId/e and III. This shows that a tendency for different fashion trends already
existed during the Aurignacian period. The pieces from the stratified layers were
recovered from all over the excavated surfaces and therefore do not allow for the
reconstruction of a division of labor during production; Ivory sticks with an oval
cross section are the initial shape of the bead production process and were found
alongside blanks, semi-finished, finished, final products and damaged pieces.
Square 25 in AH Va is an exception: Twenty-three finished pieces were found in
this square. It is possible that an object onto which the beads were fastened, such
as a belt or something similar, was lost or discarded in this area of the cave and
then decomposed. This is the best explanation for the collection of the numerous
tiny beads in this location. Diagonally across the valley lies the Sirgenstein cave.
Only one double perforated bead was found here by Robert Rudolf Schmidt, while
sorting the sediments, and was published in 1912.
The piece probably came from layer IV and is
not damaged. In contrast to the smaller pieces
from the Hohle Fels, this bead is 1.5 cm long and
relatively large.

The Geißenklösterle cave near Blaubeuren
was first discovered in 1958 and then excavated
between 1973 and 1991. Additional excavations
took place in 2001/2002. Seventeen pieces of
jewelry were recovered from the archaeological
horizons II and III. AH II dates to between 31,000
and 34,000 years ago, similarly to the mighty layer
IV in the Hohle Fels. Layer III returned the so far
oldest dates for cave find sites on the Swabian
Jura, 38,000 years before present. Three ivory
pendants were found in this oldest layer while the
remaining pieces come from layer II: The double
perforated bead also predominates at this site
and all stages of the production process can be
documented. Long and narrow ivory bands are a
specialty from this site. Three only partially preserved pieces were recovered. A perforation was
preserve on one piece, which is also decorated
with short, parallel score marks. An additional
band was found in layer III of the Hohle Fels. There
are numerous interpretations for these bands:
They may have been used as arm or ankle bands,

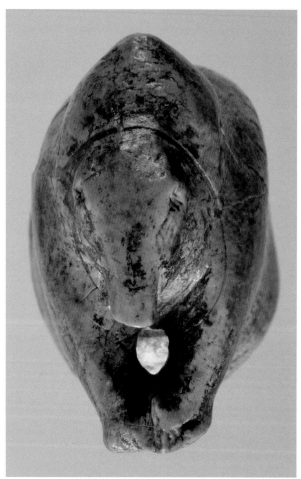

3

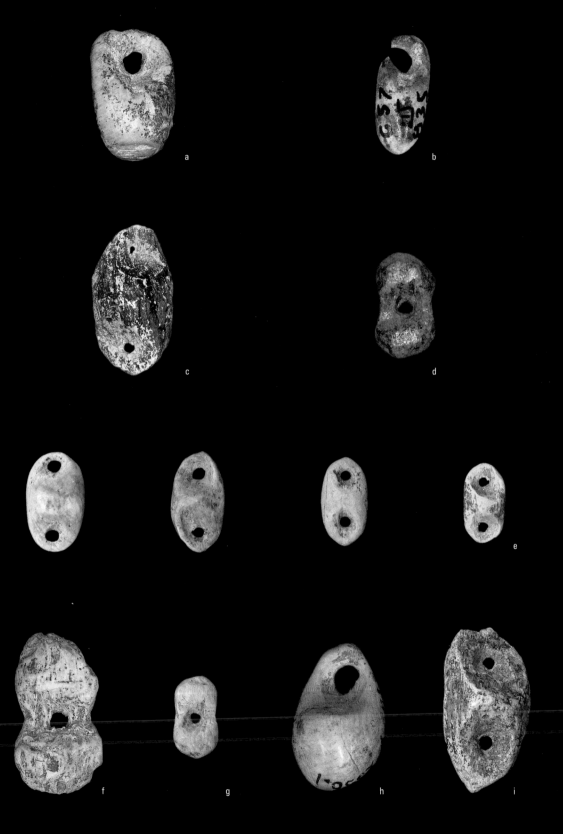

a   b   c   d   e   f   g   h   i

4

1 cm

5 Bockstein-Törle
a　half bead made out of mammoth
　　ivory
b　jewelry blank made out of
　　mammoth ivory
c　denticulated ring made out of
　　clay slate
d, e beads made out of clay slate

6 Hohle Fels. From blank to bead –
chaîne opératoire of bead making,
as evidenced through the excavated
artifacts

as a collier or a headband, or they may have been sewn onto clothing. In any case, they are personal adornments and represent another jewelry form alongside the beads and pendants made out of ivory.

The Vogelherd in the Lone Valley was excavated in 1931. The thickest layers IV and V date to between 31,000 and 36,000 years ago. Eleven world famous figurines, primarily made out of ivory were found at this site. Some of these pieces were obviously meant to be worn as pendants as is evidenced by perforations of broken eyelets. However, the excavator, Gustav Riek in 1934 only described one perforated and decorated upper eyetooth from a deer and one brown bear canine as jewelry. Between 2005 and 2012, the debris in front of the cave from the 1931 excavation was reexamined and numerous small artifacts that had been overlooked in 1931 could be recovered. These include about 350 ivory beads. The majority of these are double perforated beads, followed by single perforated beads. The former are frequently damaged yet the broken edges are often rounded and show signs of wear. They were probably lost during the activities of day-to-day life. The beads are all smaller than 0.8 cm. They were produced in series from ivory stick fragments. Although the pieces were not found in intact stratigraphic contexts, they can be placed into the Aurignacian based on comparisons with the finds from the Ach Valley caves. Also, the Aurignacian layers were the most abundant layers in the Vogelherd and 90 % of all finds were recovered from these layers. The form and shape of the finds correspond to those from the Ach Valley; however, they do not have the same range of variation.

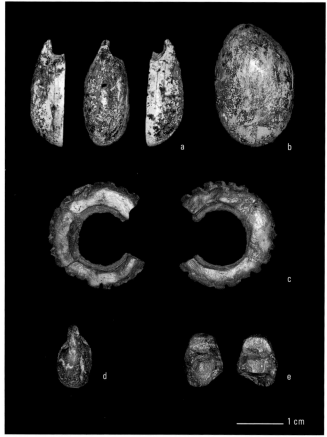

a　b

c

d　e

_____ 1 cm

5

In 1939, excavations at the Hohlenstein-Stadel recovered a basket-shaped and a globular-shaped ivory bead alongside the Lion Man figure and six fox canine teeth. An additional globular bead was found during the renewed excavations in 2009. This form is unique among the jewelry inventories of the different regions during Aurignacian in Europe. Five pieces of jewelry were found in the Bockstein-Törle in 1954. They include a blank and a damaged oval ivory bead as well as a denticulated ring made out of clay slate, a pendant and a defect blank that were also carved out of clay slate. The pieces are comparable to pieces found in the Wildscheuer cave near Steeden in Hessia and with jewelry from the open air site Lommersum in the county Euskirchen.

The double perforated bead and the knob-shaped bead found in the cave find sites of the Jura are unique to this region and nothing comparable has been found in other regions. In fact, all regions with Aurignacian inventories posess characteristic pieces of jewelry that are more or less limited to that geographic region. An additional example for this is the basket-shaped bead from Southwestern France that was limited to this area. The double perforated bead is present in all layers of the Hohle Fels on the Swabian Jura and shows that a tradition existed here for the production and use of this special form. This suggests a specific group identity for the people of the Swabian Jura, which was expressed through these identifying elements. Therefore, jewelry is not just decorative but primarily an object of communication and identification, whose meaning is understood and interpreted within a specific group.

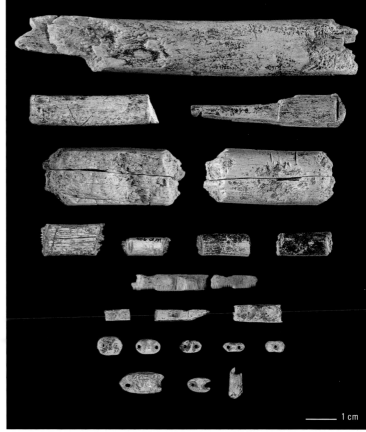

1 cm

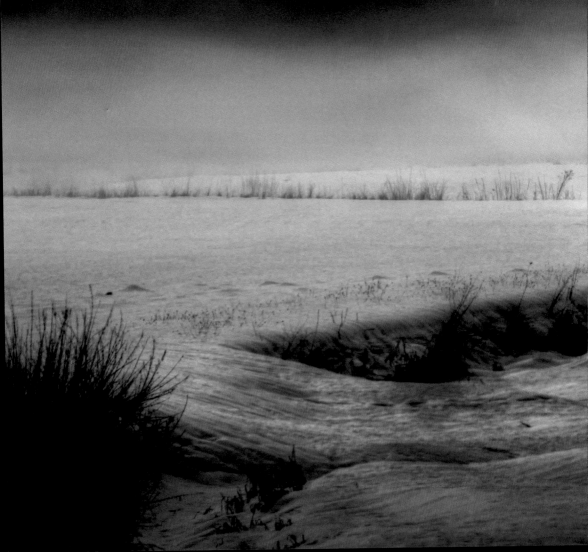

SOUNDS FROM THE PAST

FLUTES FROM THE AURIGNACIAN ON THE SWABIAN JURA

SUSANNE C. MÜNZEL
NICHOLAS J. CONARD

The oldest known musical instruments, that is to say the oldest known flutes, were found in the Ach and Lone Valley of the Swabian Jura. Flutes are differentiated from simple pipes or whistles, still used during hunting even today, through numerous finger holes that make it possible to play melodies.

The history of the flutes from the Swabian Jura is variable. The first so called "swan wing bone flute", made out of the bone from a swan wing, was discovered while sorting and analyzing faunal bones from the Geißenklösterle in 1995. The 30 Fragments were spread across three boxes from the 1990 excavation and were identified as part of a flute based on the characteristically scraped finger holes. Not all of the 30 fragments could be refit to one flute, therefore we can assume that at least two flutes made out of swan wing bones existed at

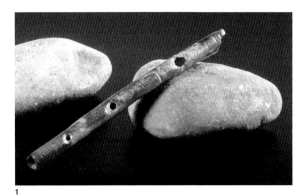

the Geißenklösterle. The third flute from this cave, the so-called "mammoth ivory flute", was also discovered years after the original excavation during an inventory of the thousands of ivory artifacts from the cave. It was previously described as a torso-fragment in Joachim Hahn's publication on the Geißenklösterle. Maria Malina recognized that the fragments were a part of a flute while trying to refit additional pieces to the ivory fragment. This flute was also fashioned with characteristically scraped finger holes.

1

The flute fragments from the Vogelherd in the Lone Valley were also identified long after they were originally excavated, 85 years earlier. The sediments from the 1931 excavation were recently re-excavated, washed and sorted by students from the Institute for Prehistory of the University at Tübingen between 2005

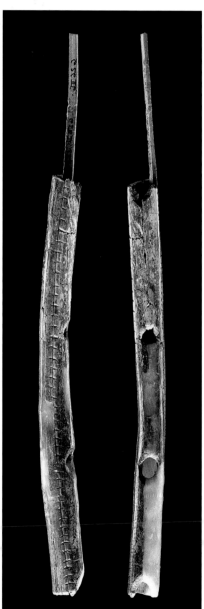

and 2012. Numerous relatively small fragments, including at least one bird bone flute and one mammoth ivory flute, were overlooked during the original excavation and were first recognized as the fragments of flutes after the finds from the Geißenklösterle were identified.

The most complete flute, the so called "vulture bone flute", was found in the Hohle Fels in 2008 and is, so far, the only specimen that was found in situ during the excavation. The flute was found 70 cm next to the "Venus from Hohle Fels", located in the lower layers of the Aurignacian period. Two additional small fragments from two separate ivory flutes were also recovered from these layers. All eight flutes from the Ach and Lone Valleys were found in Aurignacian layers and are therefore among the oldest finds made by modern man, who first migrated into the upper Danube regions ca. 40,000 years ago, in Central Europe.

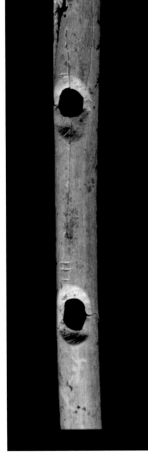

3

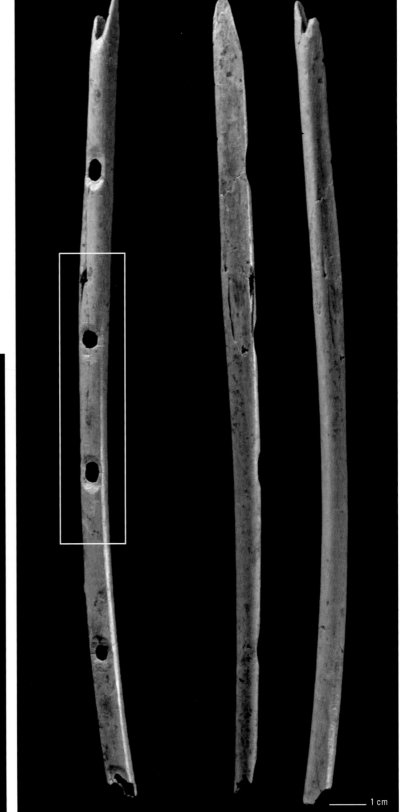

4

1 cm

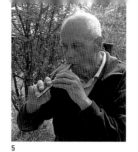

5

FLUTE
MAKING

Experimental archeology is essential in order to better understand and comprehend the past; it has become an indispensible institution in our research. Experimental reconstructions are necessary for the study of these flutes since they were not preserved intact. Although the flutes all look different, there are similarities in their construction. The two well preserved flutes made from bird bones from the Geißenklösterle and the Hohle Fels were both made from the radius (lower arm/wing bone) of the bird's wing. The other bone from the lower arm/wing, the ulna, was apparently not used to produce flutes on the Swabian Jura. That is very different in Isturitz, a find site in the French Pyrenees that is ca. 15,000 years younger than the find layers from the Swabian Jura. This site contained the remains of more than 20 flutes. These were fashioned almost exclusively from the ulna of a bird's wing, primarily from vultures. Experiments with reproduced flutes show that the two wing bones produce a different pitch and must be played differently. The ulna has a wider cross section and is easier to play. It has a slightly lower pitch while the radius has a narrower cross section, produces a higher pitch and is more difficult to play. Another characteristic element of the flutes, even the ivory flutes, is the finger holes which were scored, not drilled, using stone tools.

3, 4 Hohle Fels. Bone flute made from the radius of a griffon vulture, L 21.8 cm
5 Friedrich Seeberger playing the mammoth ivory flute (2006)

6 Reconstruction of flutes made by Friedrich Seeberger (2006):
a, b "Mammoth flute" made from the wood of an elder bush, notched flute and end-blown flute
c "Mammoth flute" made of ivory
d Isturitz flute made from the ulna of a bearded vulture
e Flute made from the ulna of a crane, Jiahu (China, ca. 6000 B.C.)
f, g "Swan flute" from the Geißenklösterle, made from the radius of a white and whooper swan
h Ulna of a white swan as a notched

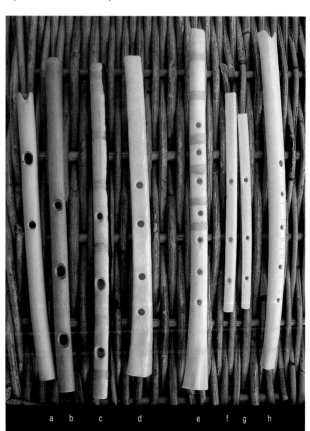

a b c d e f g h

6

PLAYING
THE FLUTES

At this point, it is important to mention Friedrich Seeberger (1938–2007); his recon-structions of the swan wing bone flute and the mammoth ivory flute, as well as his ability to play them both made him a pioneer in the field experimental archeology concerning these flutes. He based the reconstruction of the two flutes on the technique used for playing end-blown flutes, e.g. as in the Egyptian ney or shep-herd's flutes from the Mediterranean region. These flutes do not have a mouth-piece and are played by blowing diagonally across the rim of the flute opening. This method of blowing was probably also used to play the one complete flute from Isturitz, which also only has a smooth rim and no extra mouthpiece. The style of playing the ney offers a greater range of sounds, due to the freedom of move-ment of the mouth, than notched, block or cross flutes have.

The swan wing bone flute has also been reconstructed with three finger holes like the fragmented original. This reconstruction makes it possible to play a range of seven different notes without cross-fingering. It is also possible to reconstruct the flute with four finger holes to achieve a correspondingly wider range of sounds.

The vulture flute is notched at the end and was probably played differently. Wulf Hein, archeological technician, has made a playable reconstruction of this flute. The vulture bone is longer than the swan bone, which is why the original was fashioned with four complete finger holes as well as one broken hole. The anatomical length of the bone would allow for up to six finger holes.

The interest in the origins of music increases with each passing year. All the while, composers and flutists are composing and playing the various reconstructions of the earliest flutes from the Swabian Jura, thereby testing the possibilities and styles of playing mankind's oldest melodic instruments.

Victor Hugo said: "Music is noise that thinks". After I had reconstructed my first Paleolithic flute out of a swan wing bone and tried to play a few notes on it, it sounded more like the screech of a derailed train or a hissing tea kettle, definitely not like something carefully considered or thought out. That was in 1995, shortly after the discovery of the first bone flute during inventory of finds from the Geißenklösterle cave near Blaubeuren; a sensational find because it showed that the reindeer hunters of the Aurignacian of

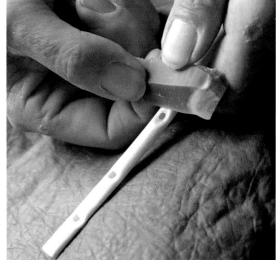

8

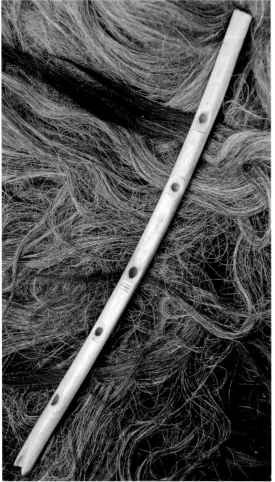

7

the Swabian Jura were obviously musical and made their own music. However, we can only know what their instruments may have sounded like through experimentation. No sooner said than done: Analysis of the marks on the original flute made it possible to reconstruct the individual steps in the production of the flutes. We now know of two types of flutes from the caves of the Swabian Jura – simple pipes made from hollow bird bones as well as pipes made out of two hollowed out halves of mammoth ivory, the finger holes are not drilled but were scored. In the past years, I have reconstructed all of the discovered flutes multiple times; however, even if it is relatively easy to build such a flute, it is much more difficult to play them. It requires a certain amount to talent and a lot of practice to make the thin column of air in the pipes resonate with sound. I am not a musician and quickly reached the limits of my musical talents. Instead, I gave the reproductions to professional flutists and they were able to produce much more harmonic results. As a result of these experiments, we now assume that the Paleolithic instruments were pentatonic and well tuned for our modern ears.

It is still not clear whether the flutes were played with some sort of mouthpiece and what this may have looked like. It is possible to play the flutes using various different techniques and further experiments will show the range of melodies that sounded through the hills and valleys of the Swabian Jura 35,000 years ago.

AGE OF THE ICE AGE ART

KURT WEHRBERGER

KURT WEHRBERGER

1 Sequence of cultures of the Upper Paleolithic in the caves of the Swabian Jura (years before present, where "present" is the year 1950). There is no evidence for human habitation from the coldest phase of the Würm glacial period in combination with the greatest glacier expansion between ca. 20,500 and 17,500 years ago

The Upper Paleolithic in Central Europe is differentiated into a sequence of cultures that are defined based on different tool inventories composed of stone, antler, bone and ivory. The designation of the cultures follows a nomenclature established in Western Europe: They are named for important find sites in France – L'Aurignac, La Gravette and La Madeleine.

The Lion Man from the Hohlenstein Stadel and the ivory figurines from the other caves of the Swabian Jura were found in layers together with tools and jewelry that are characteristic of the oldest culture of the Upper Paleolithic, the Aurignacian. One exception, the horse head from the Hohle Fels, was found in a transition area between an Aurignacian layer and the younger Gravettian. The figures from the Vogelherd were found in two different Aurignacian layers, those from the Geißenklösterle were found in the upper layer of the two identified Aurignacian horizons. These have been dated exhaustively using a series of scientific age determination methods such as radiocarbon dating (^{14}C), improved accelerator mass spectrometry (AMS) or thermoluminescence dating (TL). It is important to bear in mind that ^{14}C-dates do not represent actual calendar years. These dates need to be calibrated as a result of the heavily fluctuating ^{14}C-concentration in the atmosphere and are actually a few thousand years older.

So far it has not been possible to directly date any of the ivory figurines because ^{14}C- analyses require collagen whose concentration is too low in ivory. Animal bones, and sometimes charcoal, from the corresponding layers were primarily used to date the layers. For the most recent series of dates, researchers chose

Excursus **Radiocarbon dating**
Kurt Wehrberger

Radiocarbon dating is a technique that measures the decay of radioactive carbon (^{14}C) to estimate the age of organic materials, such as bone and wood. Radioactive carbon is created through the influence of cosmic radiation in the atmosphere. Plants, animals and humans absorb it into their organism through their metabolism. When an organism dies, the proportion of ^{14}C in the body decreases at a known constant rate: The half-life of ^{14}C is ca. 5,730 years. After this period of time, half of the radioactive carbon that an organism accrued throughout its lifetime has decayed to nitrogen. By measuring the remaining proportion of ^{14}C in the organic material it is possible to determine its age. The margin of error can, depending on the age of the sample, vary between a few decades and over 1,000 years from the actual date. The previous assumption that the proportion of ^{14}C in the atmosphere is stable was false, therefore ^{14}C-dates must be calibrated; that is to say they are compared to other methods of dating and adjusted. Dendrochronology, counting the sequence of tree rings, is used to calibrate dates from the past 14,000 years. For older periods, the dates are aligned using measurements from microorganism from deep-sea drilling cores that can also be used to determine what the climate was like in prehistoric times.

The major disadvantage of conventional ^{14}C-dating was that a large amount of sample material was needed to carry out the measurements. Sample sizes of up to 200 g were not feasible for smaller objects. In some cases, multiple objects were combined in one sample for measuring, which led to results that were probably distorted. The introduction of the AMS method (Accelerator Mass Spectrometry) made it possible to reduce the required amount of sample material to 2 g. The limit for measuring the age of an object is 40,000 to 65,000 years; older objects no longer contain measureable amounts of radioactive carbon.

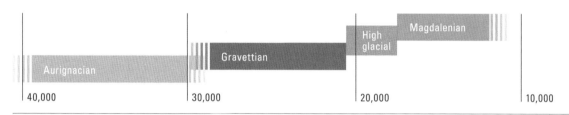

1

animal bones with cut marks for the analyses because these must have been made by human hand, e.g. while cutting up game. ^{14}C-dates also exist for the layer in which the Lion Man was found. The first conventional dating method returned an age of 32,000 years before present, later measurements using AMS dating techniques resulted in similarly old and much older dates. As a result of the new excavations from 2008 to 2013, we now have dates for the Aurignacian layers from the Stadel cave. The excavation showed that the Aurignacian horizon in the cave is composed of three separate layers. The ^{14}C –dates, based on a series of animal bones, revealed a calibrated age between 35,000 and 41,000 years. Since the Lion Man was presumably found in the lowest layer it is probably about 40,000 years old.

Taken together, the caves from the Jura contain archeological layers that give evidence for an early start and a long timespan of nearly 10,000 years for the Aurignacian period – from 40,000 to 30,000 years before present. New ^{14}C-dates from the Geißenklösterle using new methods, in which the collagen is processed using a special procedure (ultra filtration) to minimize contamination, suggest that the begin of the Aurignacian on the Swabian Jura may even extend a few thousand years further into the past.

A DIFFERENT WAY OF LIFE

CLIMATE AND ENVIRONMENT
KURT WEHRBERGER

The Quaternary period, the last of multiple major glacial periods in the Pleistocene, the youngest period of Earth's history, began 115,000 years ago and is also known as the Ice Age due to the predominance of cold periods. The Würm Ice Age, the historically and geographically developed name for the last glacial period in southern Germany, consisted of alternating warmer and colder periods. It reached its glacial maximum ca. 60,000 years ago. Afterwards, the climate became milder until 45,000 years ago with the onset of a rapid succession of more moderate and colder periods that culminated in a second, even more extreme glacial maximum ca. 20,000 year ago.

During the periods of greatest glaciations, the high glacial period, glaciers and ice shields covered large portions of Europe, including Scandinavia, northern Germany and Russia. These also enclosed the mountainous regions such as the Alps, where only the tips peaked out from the up to 700 meter thick sheets of compacted snow and ice. The average yearly temperatures sank well below zero degrees Celsius. A significant amount of water remained locked up in the snow and ice masses, therefore the world-wide sea levels were up to 100 m lower than today's levels. The coastline and the overall shape of Europe looked very different from what we are familiar with today. The British Isles, for example, were connected to the European continent and it was possible to walk there without getting one's feet wet.

Precipitation fell primarily on the large sheets of ice in Northern Europe and the alpine glaciers, as a result, the landscapes in between were not covered in ice were characterized by a cold but relatively dry climate. There was hardly any snow, even during the winters. Large portions of these landscapes were covered by grassland steppe. The spectrum of animals and plants living there resembles today's arctic tundra, but could also be compared to the African savannas. A comparable "Ice Age" manifestation cannot be found anywhere on earth today.

The climate of the Swabian Jura during the early phase of the Upper Paleolithic, 40,000 to 30,000 years ago, was not as drastic as during the glacial maximum ca. 20,000 years ago, throughout which we are missing all evidence for the presence of human beings on the Jura for thousands of years. The analysis of faunal bones recovered from the caves implies that the climate was moderate and cold. The Jura plateau was open grassland with numerous herbs and small bushes such as dwarf birch, willow, pine and berry bushes in the more sheltered areas. Open forests characterized the floodplains in the valleys with medium height trees such as birch, alder, willow and hazel bushes. The steep, rocky slopes were woodless and covered with grasses, herbs, ferns and lichens.

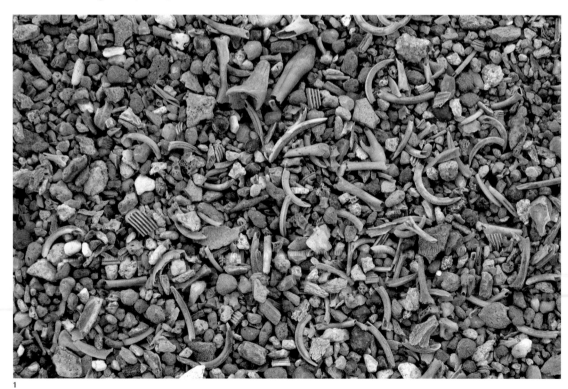

2 Reindeer on the Yamal peninsula in Western Siberia (1993). The vegetation includes dwarf birch, alpine grey willow and sedges and is comparable to the tundra during the colder periods of the last Ice Age

Large, primarily cold-period mammals such as mammoths, wooly rhinoceros, steppe bison, wild horse and reindeer subsisted mainly on the vegetation on the plateau. Deer and roe deer preferred the open forests of the floodplains. Ibex and chamois found their ideal living conditions on the rocky valley slopes. Carnivores such as wolves, foxes and lions as well as the scavenging cave hyenas hunted the herbivores. Cave bears inhabited the temperate and frost-free caves during the winters to hibernate. The large quantity of bear bones

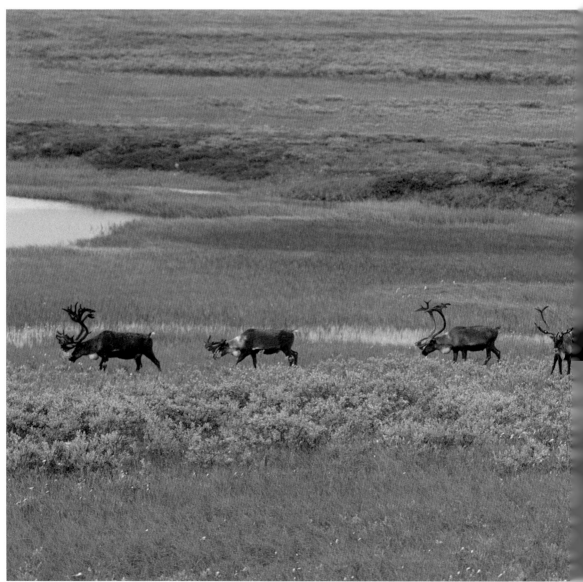

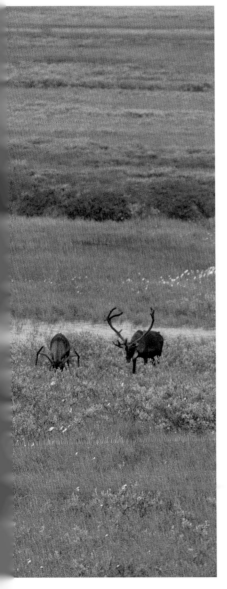

from inside the caves comes from animals that died in their sleep from sickness, weakness or old age. Young animals that were born in December or January during the hibernation period also frequently did not survive the cold season. The finds from the Hohle Fels suggest that, at times, humans also hunted cave bears. However, the primary hunting game for humans were the animals that moved in great herds such as the mammoths, wild horses, bison and reindeer. Smaller animals such as rabbits, birds and fish supplemented the human diet. There is no evidence for the presence of cave bears and cave hyenas after the last glacial maximum in Central Europe. Most of the remaining animals returned to the Jura. As the climate began to warm up toward the end of the last Ice Age, the glacial fauna either died out or migrated into colder regions in the north.

MAN AND MAMMOTH

IVORY AS A RAW MATERIAL
SIBYLLE WOLF

The woolly mammoth (Mammuthus primigenius) is extinct today; evidence shows that it lived in its classic form from the start of the last Ice Age, ca. 115,000 years ago, until the climate began to warm about 10,000 years ago, when it migrated from Central Europe towards the north east. Dwarf mammoths lived on the Siberian Wrangel island until about 5.500 years ago. Mammoth tusks were made out of ivory and grew continuously throughout the animal's lifespan. They were located in long alveoles that reached from the nostril to the root of the trunk. Up to one fourth of the trunk was imbedded in the alveole. Since tusks did not have roots like teeth, they sat on top of a cone-shaped tooth germ in the mandible. Mammoth calves had tiny deciduous tusks prior to developing the massive adult tusks. They were about 4 cm long, including the root,

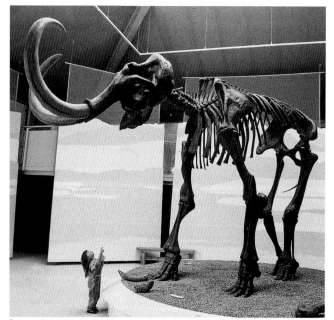

1

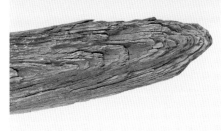

2

erupted after about 6 months and were replaced with permanent tusks after about one year. The tusks could grow between 3.5 and 15 cm per year, depending on the available food resources and the health of an animal. Until the age of five, the tusks grew more or less straight and then curved outwards before twisting backwards in later age; they could even cut across each other in especially large specimens. Each tooth grew individually and no two pairs of tusks were identical. The tusks of male animals were larger than those of female animals. They could grow up to 4.9 meters in length and weigh up to 150 kg. On average, the curved teeth reached about 2.5 meters in length and weighed circa 45 kg. The tusks of female mammoths grew to an average 1.6 meters in length and weighed about 11 kg.

The surface of the teeth is often scratched and shows evidence of wear and tear. The animals used their tusks to search the ground for food; this caused the under-side of the teeth to become unusually smooth and polished but also damaged. This may also have caused the tip of the tusk to break off. However, it may also have broken off during fights with other animals. The tusk, similarly to teeth, is built up in layers: dental cement, dentin and a pulp cavity. The pulp cavity supplies the tooth. In full-grown animals, the pulp cavity can account for up to a third of the internal volume of the tusk. The nerves run from the end of the pulp cavity to the tip of the tooth. The cone-shaped cross-section of the tooth, when cut open lengthwise, shows that it grows in growth spurts. Figuratively speaking, the tusk is built up of numerous cone-shaped layers of dentine that are imposed onto each other.

1 Mammoth skeleton. The specimen was found in 1975 at Siegsdorf near Traun-stein (Oberbayern) and had a shoulder height of 3.6 m   **2** Longitudinal cut through a mammoth tusk   **3** Stuttgart-Bad Cannstatt 1993, Recovery of a mammoth tusk. The 3.5 meter long tooth was still in its anatomical context in the mandible. Below it lay the upper leg bones, a pelvis and upper arm bones of the mammoth   **4** Geißenklösterle, deciduous teeth from mammoth calves

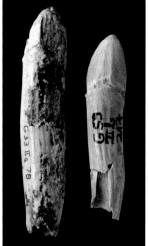

4

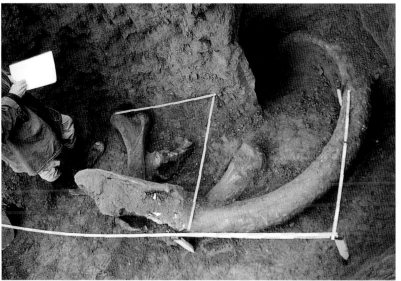

3

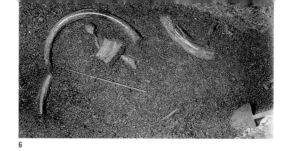

6

The youngest layers are located on the inside of the tooth, the oldest layers are located on the outside. A cross-section of the tusk shows this growth sequence as a series of concentric circles. These are called "Owen's Rings". However, the tusk is not always filled evenly with dentin: Young animals' tusks are hollow almost to the tip, dentine fills the tooth with age. The outer layer of the tooth is made up of the tooth cement. This material is bone-like and very dense. The heaviness of the cement layer varies throughout the tooth between 5 and 8 mm thickness. The hardest part of the tusk is the tooth cement at the very tip; however, it is quickly worn away and rarely preserved. Ivory is made up out of ca. 60 % dentin and the protein collagen (30 %) as well as 10 % water. Odontoblastic cells line the pulp cavity and produce the dentin. The grain of the ivory, best seen in cross section, is characteristic for mammoth ivory and can be observed with the naked eye. The intersecting growth lines are called "Schreger lines". They are the product of the varying collagen levels in the dentin and the three-dimensional arrangement of the dentin canals. The Schreger structure is genetic and characteristic for each species of elephant. The teeth and tusks of other animals are also called ivory, however, they do not display Schreger structures and are not addressed as "real" ivory. These include walrus, narwhale or warthog tusks as well as hippopotamus or sperm whale teeth.

Mammoths lived in Europe throughout the Upper Paleolithic. However, evidence shows that access to these animals – whether as prey or as a source for collecting raw materials such as bone and ivory – was only guaranteed in Central and Eastern Europe. The mammoth ivory from the Swabian Jura was primarily collected. After procuring the material it needed to be disassembled in order to make objects from it. If we assume that tusks were found in

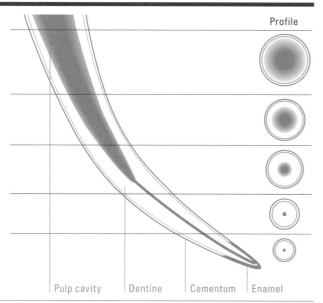

Profile

Pulp cavity   Dentine   Cementum   Enamel

5

Excursus **Paleolithic instrument making – Splitting ivory for the construction of the flute from the Geißenklösterle**

Maria Malina

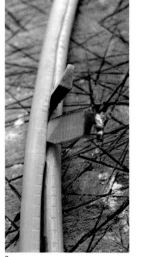

The discovery of the ca. 35,000 year old ivory flute from the Geißenklösterle in 2004 was a small sensation. Up until the discovery, the previously recovered ivory objects such as points, ivory jewelry or figurative art were only worked superficially. The known flutes were made from the long bones of birds, which are naturally hollow. In contrast, the ivory flute was made from a 19 cm long massive piece of slightly curved ivory. Archeologists were especially interested in how the flute was made.

A continuous seem could be identified during the reconstruction of the flute from 31 individual fragments: This seem shows that the ivory staff was initially split into two halves. The halves were hollowed out and then refit. Splitting using cleavers is the plausible technique for dividing a rounded staff of this length and curvature.

To prove this theory, we started an experimental trial since there is no archeological evidence for this technique of splitting from the Aurignacian, The ivory used in this experiment came from a ca. 10,000 year old tusk from Siberia. In the original flute, one half was made of tooth cement, the other from dentin. The sample for our experiment was chosen accordingly. The rounded staff was notched 2 mm deep along the cement-dentin border to create a predetermined breaking point. Afterwards, small perpendicular marks were scored into the ivory along this notched line. Their probable function was to help fix the two halves of the flute after they were hollowed out. Two small ivory cleavers were used to successfully split the ivory staff along the predetermined breaking line. We were able to split a 37 cm long piece of ivory in the experiment. In principle it is possible to split any length of ivory using this technique.

7

1. Notching

2. Setting a wedge

3. Rounding

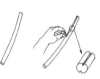

4. Create a breaking line

5. Scoring

6. Cleave

7. Cleaving, continued

8. Cleaved pieces

9. Smoothing

10. Fitting

11. Hollowing out

12. Creation of the finger holes

13. Gluing/binding

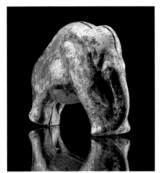

10

their anatomical position, then the tusk had to first be removed from the bone either by smashing it with heavy stones or by using a pick to remove the bone from the root-end of the tusk. Afterwards the tusks were broken down into smaller fragments or split lengthwise. Another method required the tooth to be notched all around in order to then break or cut a segment of the tusk. After fragmenting the tusk, it possible to cut grooves into the material to form long, narrow bands of ivory that serve as blanks for further processing. The blanks are then formed into the desired product by chipping, carving, shaving, grinding, smoothing or polishing them. Ivory was predominantly used to make jewelry but also points, figurines and special objects such as flutes or spatulas. On the one hand, ivory is the only material available from which to carve large figurines, but it was certainly also appreciated for its dense and fine structure, light color and pleasing aesthetics as well as for its sensory stimuli.

The Russian sites recorded an especially rich mammoth ivory industry and numerous figurines. The Don region is known for huts that were constructed out of mammoth bones and tusks. The mammoth played a central role in the lives of Paleolithic hunters and gatherers. About 400 mammoth representations, including figurines, reliefs, engravings and cave paintings, are known today. The majority of these representations are engravings and paintings such as the ones found in the Grotte Chauvet or in Rouffignac in Southern France. The oldest figurative depictions of mammoths were carved out of mammoth ivory and were found at the 40,000 year old sites of the Swabian Jura.

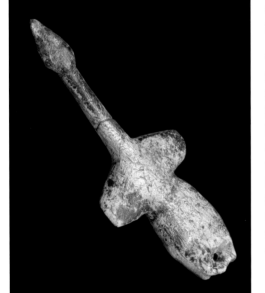

9

Excursus **Flute sounds and mammoth teeth – The experimental production of a flute made out of mammoth ivory**

Angela Holdermann, Johannes Wiedmann, Frank Trommer

Flutes are among the oldest musical instruments created by mankind. Ca. 40,000 years ago, flutes were primarily fashioned from the long bones of birds and a few specimens were also made out of mammoth ivory. In contrast to the naturally hollow long bones, a suitable piece of ivory needed to first be prepared from the tusk. Secondly, the piece needed to be split lengthwise, then the halves were hollowed out and, finally, holes were added. Only then were the two halves fitted together to form a flute. We were interested

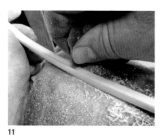

in how long it would take to fashion such a complex instrument. We asked ourselves the following questions: Did the flute makers use fresh or sub-fossilized ivory? There is evidence to suggest that the Paleolithic flute makers

11

were forced to use subfossilized ivory like we do today. What is the best temperature at which ivory can be worked? Attempts to split ivory at subzero temperatures were relatively successful. Faults in

the material itself prevented a clean division of the two halves. We also compared if there are difference when working with dry or watered ivory. As a matter of fact, it was easier to work with ivory that was previously soaked in water. We used narrow flint scrapers as well as the incisors from large rodent, e.g. from groundhogs, to hollow out the two halves of the flute. It turns out that these were ideal for this kind of work. Five finger holes and the blowhole were added before the two halves were fit together and fastened using sinew fibers and birch tar. In sum, it took us (inexperience ivory workers) 13.5 hours to fashion a playable flute out of mammoth ivory.

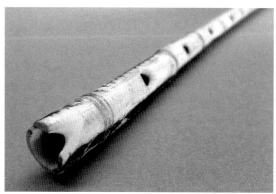

12

Fresh ivory without tears or fissures can best be processed if it has first been frozen. In contrast, fossil ivory is best processed after soaking it in water and can then be carved just like wood. In contrast to ivory from the Asian (Elephas maximus) and African Elephants (Loxodonta africana), nowadays it is legal to work with fossil mammoth ivory. The living animals were protected in 1975 and 1989 through CITES (Convention on International Trade in Endangered Species of Wild Fauna and Flora). Mammoth ivory trade is legal and has been continued for centuries. Between 1809 and 1910, more than 6,000 tons of mammoth ivory were salvaged in Siberia and sold. The demand for ivory is still strong today. Today, the local residents of Siberia have specialized in searching for mammoth tusks in the Siberian permafrost during the summer months. In Germany, ivory artists produce high quality objects. The processing of this valuable raw material has a 40,000 year old tradition.

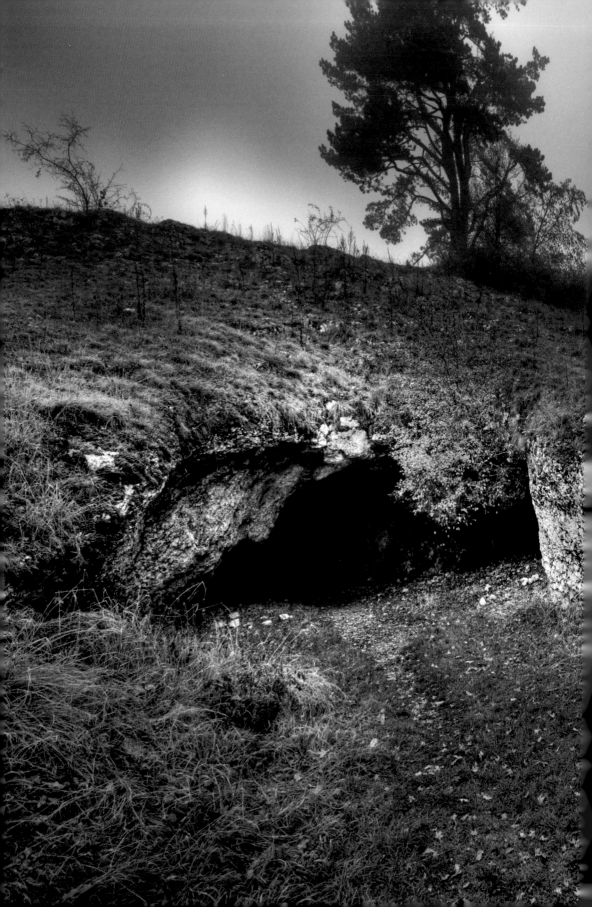

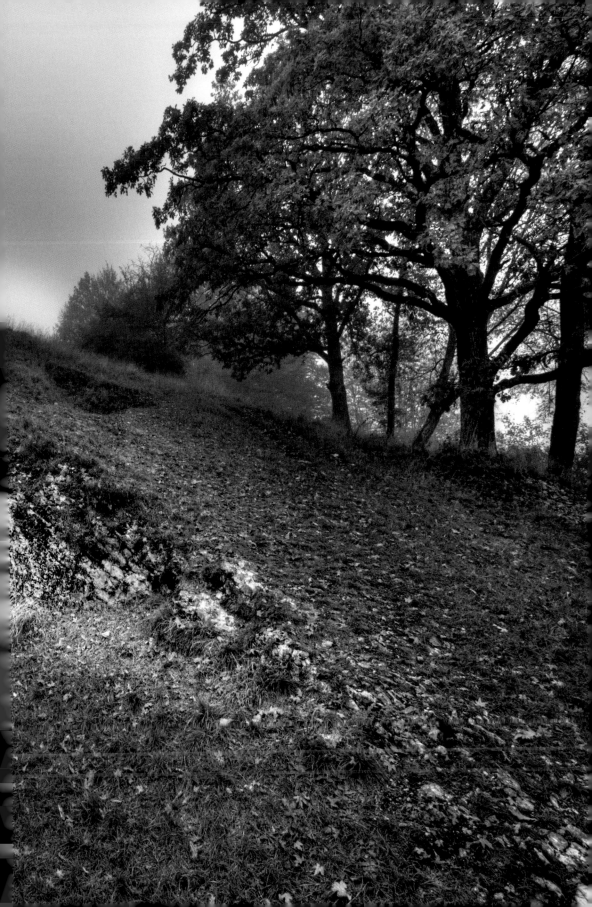

THE CAVE LION

REINHARD ZIEGLER

In the early Middle Pleistocene, circa 800,000 years ago, the lion (Panthera leo), originating in Africa, reached Europe. The cave lion from the Late Pleistocene carries the scientific name Panthera leo spelaea. He owes his name to the fact that his remains were most frequently found and preserved within cave sediments. The remains usually consist of a few bones or teeth. Complete skulls are less frequent and skeletons or even partial skeletons are extremely rare. Many of the caves from the Swabian and Franconian Jura also contained the remains of cave lions: Hohlenstein, Vogelherd and Bockstein in the Lone Valley, Charlottenhöhle and Irpfelhöhle, Hohle Fels and Brillenhöhle, Aufhauser cave, Sibyllenhöhle, Große

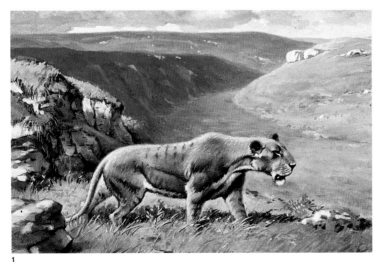

1

Ofnet and Zoolithenhöhle near Burggailenreuth. The holotype skull, the skull used for the first description of the species by George August Goldfuss in 1810, was originally found in the Zoo-lithenhöhle. The cave lion finds all date to the last Ice Age. However, lions lived in Europe prior to this, during glacial as well as during interglacial phases. They all belong to the species Panthera leo, the same species as the lions still living in the present. The oldest known remains of lions in Germany come from the early Middle Pleistocene, the Mosbachium. This early lion was very large and is called Panthera leo fossilis. The carnassial shear, a very effective slicer, much like a pair of scissors between the last pre-molars and molars, used to cut and slice flesh, was not as evolved as in Panthera leo fossilis, the later cave lions and to lions living today. In southern Germany, the faunal inventories from Mauer, Mosbach 2 and Obrigheim/Neckar contained remains from this early species. The remains of lions were found among the interglacial antiquus gravel as well as the following glacial trogontherii-primigenius pebbles in Steinheim/Murr. The skull is narrower and shorter than the skull of cave lions. The meager lion remains from the Heppenloch and from the Middle Pleistocene travertine at Stuttgart-Bad Cannstatt cannot be assigned to one subspecies due to inadequate preservation of the bones.

The descent of the cave lion (Panthera leo spelaea) from Panthera leo fossilis is undisputed. Helmut Hemmer, zoologist at the University of Mainz, showed that the evolution followed a line from West and Central Europe toward Eastern Europe with local influences on the transformation of the species. The real cave lion first appeared in the Upper

2

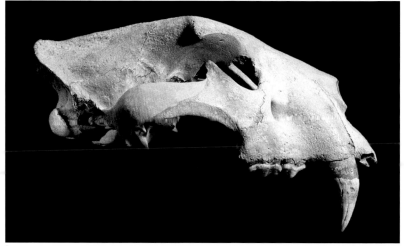

3

Pleistocene. It was smaller than its ancestor but larger than lions today. Finds from the last interglacial travertine in Thuringia and Stuttgart-Untertürkheim are evidence for this development. The documentation is better during the last Ice Age. The remains of cave lions were found at the mentioned cave sites as well as at open-air sites such as, for example, the loess from the quaternary in Stuttgart.

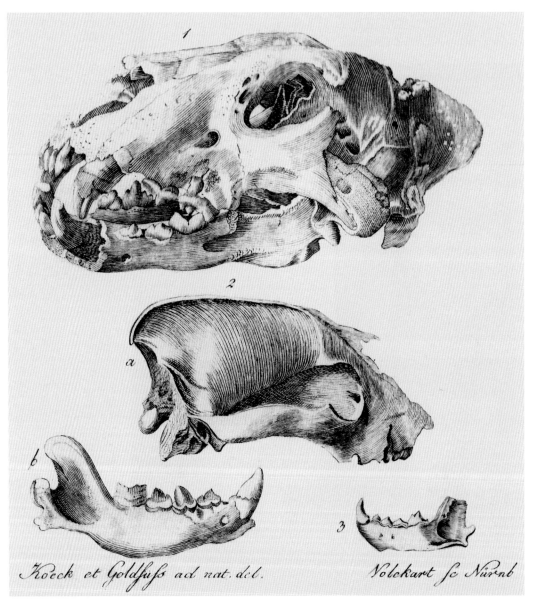

Koeck et Goldfuß ad nat. del.   Volckart sc Nürnb

The gravel quarries of the Upper Rhine Rift are an abundant source for the remains of fossil lions, including cave lions. The partial skeleton from Huttenheim is especially noteworthy. The complete skeleton of a cave lion, found in 1985 in the Gerhartsreiter Rift near Siegsdorf, is especially interesting because it shows evidence of having been manipulated by humans. Carin Gross examined the skeleton and reported cut and score marks on the ribs, hip bone and upper leg bones that prove that humans must have removed flesh from the bones.

In the Pleistocene, lions ranged from Europe to the Taimyr Peninsula in northern Siberia and China. They crossed the Bering Strait and even reached North and South America. The cave lion became extinct in Southern Germany by the end of the paleolithic period about 11,000 years ago. The youngest finds come from the Zigeunerfels near Sigmaringen.

Genetic analyses on recent as well as fossil lions by Joachim Burger (Molecular Archeology, University of Mainz) and colleagues show that the cave lions are more closely related to today's lions than to any other Pantherinae. Therefore, the cave lion is not a cave tiger as speculated by Theodor Groiss on the basis of a comparison of brain casts. The rareness of the cave lion finds led to the supposition that the animal was a loner and therefore must be a cave tiger. There are no secure Holocene finds of lions north of the Alps. In the Balkan and in Asia Minor, lions existed into historical periods and some can also be identified as cave lions. It is not sure that the Holocene lions of southern Europe are the direct descendents of cave lions. Today, lions only live in parts of Africa south of the Sahara. One small isolated population exists in the Gir reservation in India. The relic areas are only a small portion of the much larger dispersal area that once stretched from Africa across the Near East and Asia Minor into India up until the Holocene.

4 Skull of a cave lion from the Zoolithenhöhle near Burggailenreuth. From the publication by Georg August Goldfuss 1810

5 Skeleton of a cave lion from the Natural History and Mammoth Museum in Siegsdorf

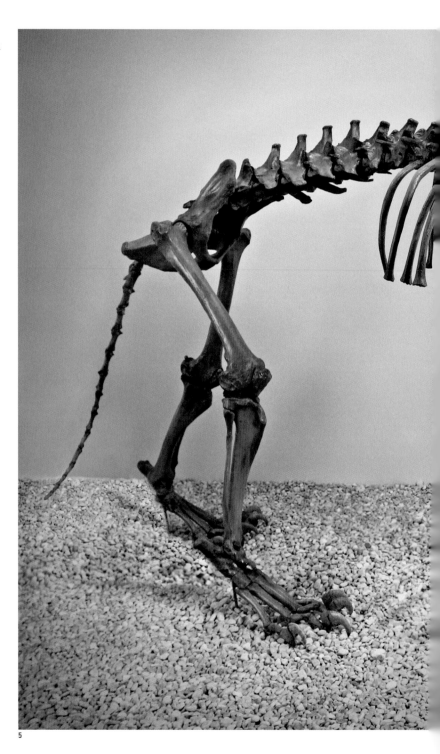

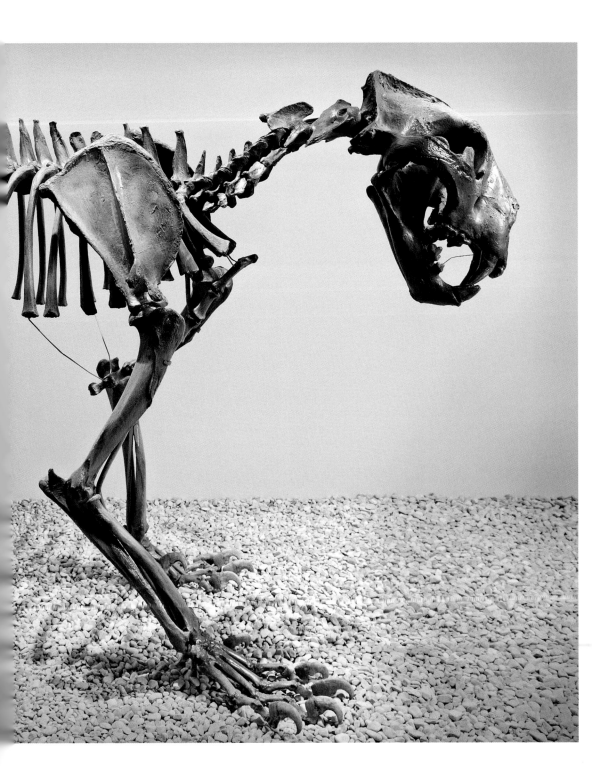

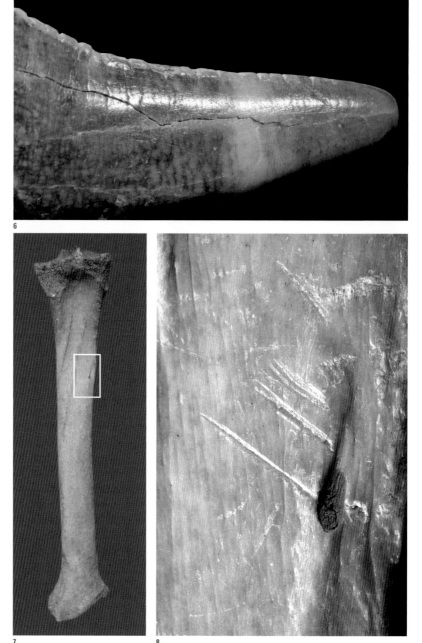

6 Hohle Fels. Canine of a cave lion with a notched tooth crown   **7, 8** Hohle Fels. Cut marks on the shinbone of a cave lion   **9, 10** Hohle Fels. Canine of a cave lion from the Aurignacian layer that was used as a retoucher

6

7   8

The name cave lion is deceptive since the large cats, contrary to the cave bears, never lived or hibernated in caves. As meat eaters (carnivores), cave lions were able to survive the winter with sufficient meat for food while cave bears, who were vegetarian, could only survive the cold periods with a relatively long hibernation period inside the caves. Numerous cave lion bones were regularly found among the huge number of cave bear bones recovered from the caves of the Swabian Jura. For example, eighteen bones and seven teeth from cave lions were found in the Hohle Fels near Schelklingen. Ten of these show evidence of having been manipulated by humans. Cut marks on the bones prove that cave lions were also hunted and butchered. The location of the cut marks on the shinbones of the lion is evidence that the big cats were not just hunted for their pelts as the ivory figurine of the Lion Man suggests. It is strange that no jewelry made from the cats' canine teeth has been found on the Swabian Jura. Tools made from the canines, so called retouchers or pressure flakers for finishing stone tools, are much more frequent. The front and backside of the retouchers show deep depressions on both sides of the tooth root caused by working with the tool. However, the canine with carved notches on the crown is unique. The traces of human activities on the lion bones suggest that the lions, although they were revered as evidenced by the ivory figurine of the Lion Man, were also hunted, eaten and their teeth used as tools, just like other prey animals were.

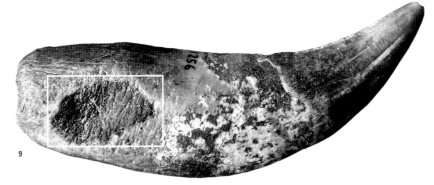

9

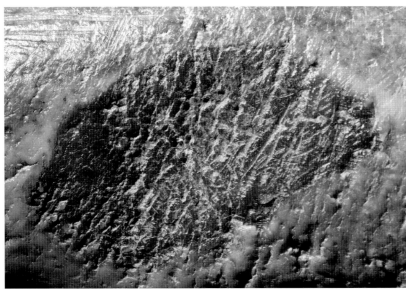

10

BIG CATS
IN PALEOLITHIC ART
KURT WEHRBERGER

As the cave explorers entered the unknown cave in the Ardèche Valley through a narrow crevice in December 1994, they did not know that they were about to discover an archeological sensation. The discovery of the Grotte Chauvet near Vallon-Pont-d'Arc was the most important discovery of a Paleolithic painted cave of the past decades. The aesthetic quality and sophisticated technique of the majority of the representations as well as the variety of over 400 black and red painted or engraved animal representations are simply stunning.

About forty lions were depicted among the representations of the Grotte Chauvet, by far the most representations of big cats known from any painted cave to date. The depictions are usually quite rare. The sequence and superposition of some pictures suggest that they are supposed to depict an individual animal in different stages of motion – from alert and lurking to threatening and aggressive. None of the animals have a mane, yet some of them were clearly painted with male genitalia. This suggests that it was not possible to differentiate the sex of an Ice Age lion based on the presence of a mane, which is present in most modern male lions after four or five years of age. The cave also contains the only known representation of a leopard,

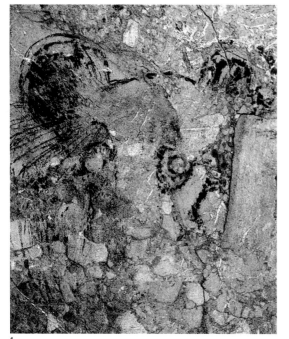

1

one of the smaller big cats that are only rarely documented among the faunal bone inventories from the last Ice Age. The largest and strangest lion depicted in painted caves was found in La Baume-Latrone near Nîmes. The stylized figure is three meters long and is the central animal in a larger composition that also includes mammoths and horses. The drawing was originally interpreted as a reptile or some other fantastic creature; it is reduced to show a powerful head with wide open jaws and terrifying fangs while the body is only made up of a few curved lines. Impressive depictions of lions are also known from the famous painted caves Lascaux in the Dordogne or Les Trois Frères in the Pyrenees. The lion depictions from these caves were mostly dated to the later Upper Paleolithic (Magdalenian). The age for the paintings of the Grotte Chauvet is still the subject of debate. Radio-carbon dates from charcoal from the paintings themselves, from traces left by torches and from fragments collected from the cave floor near the paintings vary between 25,000 and 31,000 years. Therefore, the oldest paintings date to the Aurignacian period. However, other tests delivered younger dates, placing the paintings into the Gravettian or the Magdalenian. The debate concerning the applied dating techniques and stylistic arguments, which speak for a younger

1 Les Trois Frères (Ariège). Head of a lion, H ca. 50 cm   **2** La Baume-Latrone (Gard). Lions and two mammoths, L max. ca. 300 cm

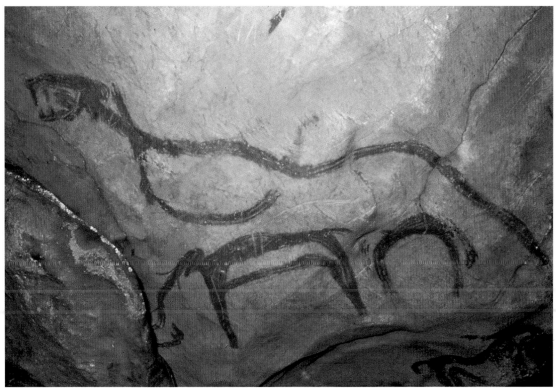

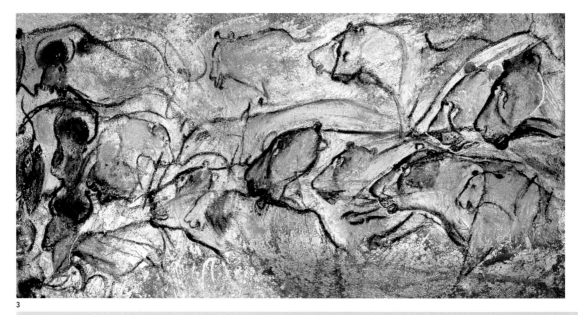

3

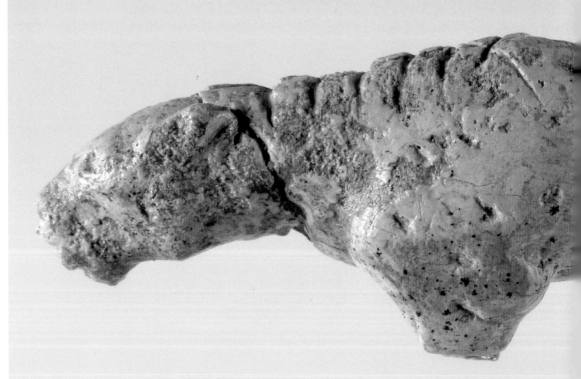

4

age of the paintings, continue to complicate the precise chronological classification of the Grotte Chauvet. The depictions of lions in figurative art, this includes decorated objects of daily use, jewelry and objects such as small figurines, can be differentiated geographically as well as chronologically. The lion representations from the Czech open air sites Dolní Věstonice and Pavlov date to the middle phase of the Upper Paleolithic, comparable to the Gravettian. These sites included numerous animal figurines, among them multiple small lion heads, which were formed out of clay and then burned. The inventory also includes the simple, yet powerful silhouette of a lion carved out of ivory that is depicted in a lurking

3 Grotte Chauvet (Rhône-Alpes). Section of the lion panel. It either depicts a pack of lions or a study in motion of one individual animal   **4** Vogelherd. Lion, ivory, L 6.8 cm   **5** La Vache (Ariège). "Panel of lions", bone, L 17.2 cm

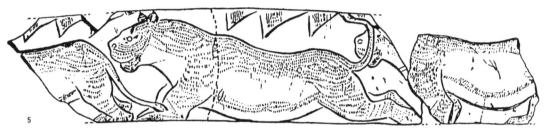

5

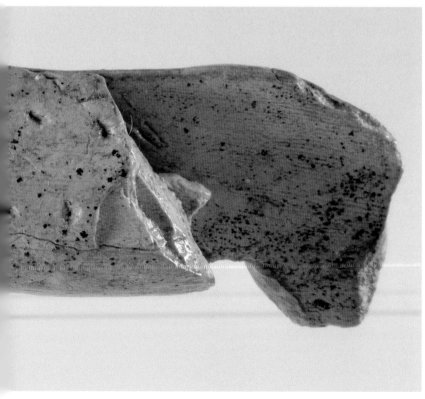

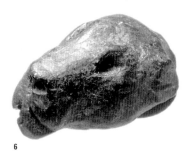

6

position, ready to pounce. Lion representations from the Pyrenean caves Gourdan,
Isturitz and La Vache date to the late Upper Paleolithic, the Magdalenian. In
Gourdan, the lion is depicted indirectly in the form of to paw prints on a decorated
staff made from reindeer antler: The complex representation also includes horses,
animal heads, symbols and animal tracks. The famous „panel of lions" was found
in the La Vache cave. Three lions, each one in a different poise, were carved in
succession on a piece of bone.

The oldest known lions in Paleolithic art were found in the Vogelherd cave in
the Lone Valley. In sum, seven more or less fragmented lion figurines made out
of mammoth ivory were discovered during the excavations from 1931 and the
renewed excavations between 2005 and 2012. Although the sculptures from
the renewed excavations were found in the material previously excavated in the
1930s and cannot be assigned to a specific stratigraphic layer, they can be
assigned to the Aurignacian period. Only three of them can be clearly identified
as depictions of big cats, one of these is the fragmented head, preserved as
two fragments, of a lion – its contours and the details bear a striking resemblance
to the head of the Lion Man from the Stadel cave.

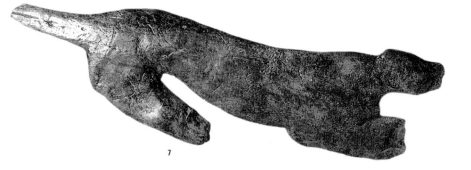

7

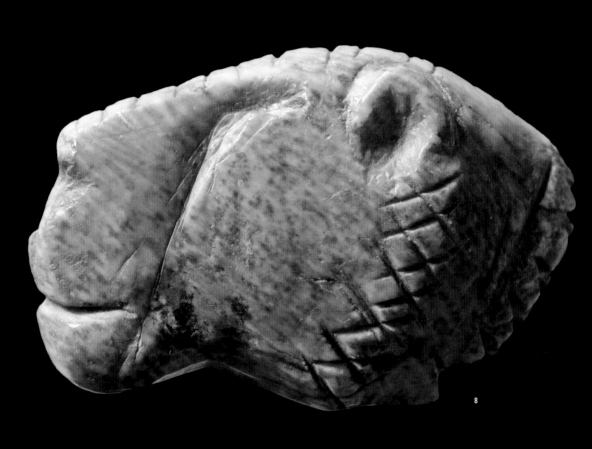

8

THE VENUS OF HOHLE FELS

AND HUMAN DEPICTIONS OF THE AURIGNACIAN
NICHOLAS J. CONARD

1 Hohle Fels. Female fugurine (Venus), ivory, H 6.0 cm

Until fairly recently conventional wisdom suggested that the Aurignacian art of the Swabian Jura was almost exclusively dedicated to the depiction of animals. The most famous exception to this rule was the enigmatic Lion Man from Hohlenstein-Stadel, which stood out due to its content and unusual size. The only other images to be considered in any way human were the so-called anthopomorphic carving from Gustav Riek's excavation in 1931 at Vogelherd and the small therianthropic relief of a mixed human-animal from Joachim Hahn's excavation at Geißenklöster-le. In contrast to these few depictions that were at most partly human, the region had produced numerous examples of carefully carved lions, mammoths, bison, horses, bears and other animals that were difficult to identify more specifically.

This situation changed in 2002 with the discovery of the miniature Lion Man from Hohle Fels, and still more radically in 2008 when excavators working in the basal Aurignacian deposits at Hohle Fels recovered nine carved pieces of mammoth ivory. These finds, which were recovered almost exactly 100 years after the discovery of most famous image in Paleolithic art, the Venus of Willendorf, could be refitted to form a voluptuous headless woman, which has become known as the "Venus of Hohle Fels". These discoveries showed that therianthropes and even human depictions form an important part of the corpus of figurative art during the Swabian Aurignacian.

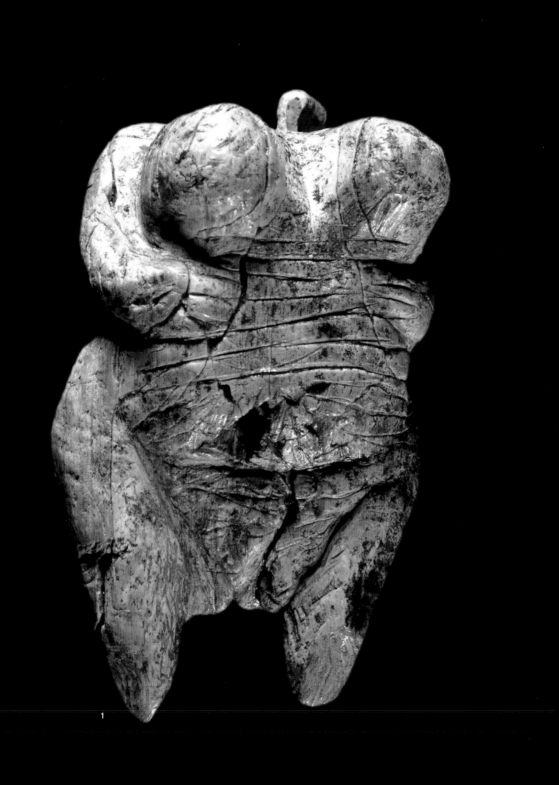

2 Hohle Fels. Overview of the excavation in the basal Aurignacian layers of Hohle Fels at the time the female figurine was discovered   **3** Stratzing. Human depiction, schist, H 7.2 cm. The excavator interpretes the figurine as a dancing woman

These depictions mainly date to the period between 35,000 and 40,000 years ago and belong to the earliest examples of figurative art known worldwide. Other human depictions from this period or slightly later are known from other regions of Europe. These include the monochrome red painting of a therianthropic "shaman" on a piece of limestone from Fumane Cave in northern Italy, the small dancing figurine carved from schist from the site of Stratzing in the Wachau, a combined depiction of a woman and a bison from Grotte Chauvet in the Ardèche of southern France, and engravings of vulvas from several Aurignacian sites in southwestern France. While all of these images differ from the Swabian examples of humans and theriothropic in their specific features, they do demonstrate that human depictions, particularly female imagery and therianthropes played a key role in the iconography of the Aurignacian and Proto-Aurignacian. Although on the whole animals are the most common subjects depicted in the ealiest art in Europe, female sexuality and fecundity and the transformations between humans and animals are also essential themes of the earliest art.

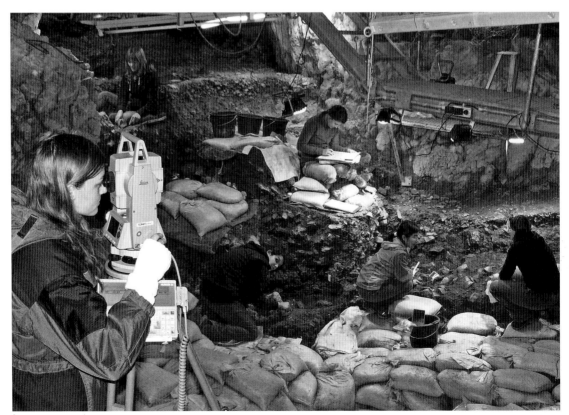

2

What is also noteworthy is the observation that figurative art of each region varies dramatically, thereby documenting multiple traditions in different media. Many scholars have pointed to the stylistic similarities between the magnificent depictions of animals, most notably lions, mammoths, horses, bears and bisons in Grotte Chauvet and the caves of the Swabian Jura, but the media used in the two regions could not be more different. The paintings from Grotte Chauvet often depict complex reditions of scenes from the Ice Age using pigments, engravings and shading to optimally use the geometry and how light from fires, lamps or torches would fall on the cave walls. In contrast, the figurines from the Swabian caves are nearly always carved from mammoth ivory. The simplistic red paintings on movable fragments of limestone from Fumane reflect a completely different tradition as does the isolated find from Stratzing and the many engravings from the Aurignacian of southwestern France.

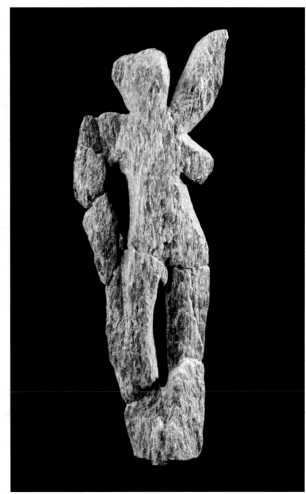

Thus, the earliest depictions of figurative art in general and the human imagery more particularly reflect distinctive creative traditions that bear only loose links to each other. The main exception to this pattern is seen in the connections in the subject matter and naturalistic imagery of Grotte Chauvet and the caves of the Ach and Lone Valleys. Many hypotheses have be put forward to try to explain the meaning of Aurignacian art, yet it is highly unlikely that one model could explain the many diverse aspects of the earliest art. While David Lewis William's popular shamanism model, Joachim Hahn's Kraft und Aggression model and other points of view have contributed to our understanding of Aurignacian art, all of these models have limitations and work best when applied to a subset of the known images. The discovery of the female figurine from Hohle Fels radically changed the discourse over the meaning of Aurignacian art by extending the Venus imagery so closely associated with the Gravettian period back roughly 10,000 years to the beginning of the Aurignacian. This discovery also moved the much debated hypotheses related to fertility into the forefront of Aurignaican art. Furthermore

4 Grotte Chauvet. Painting combining characteristic features of a woman and a bison.   **5** Vogelherd. Anthropomorphic figurine, ivory, H 6.9 cm

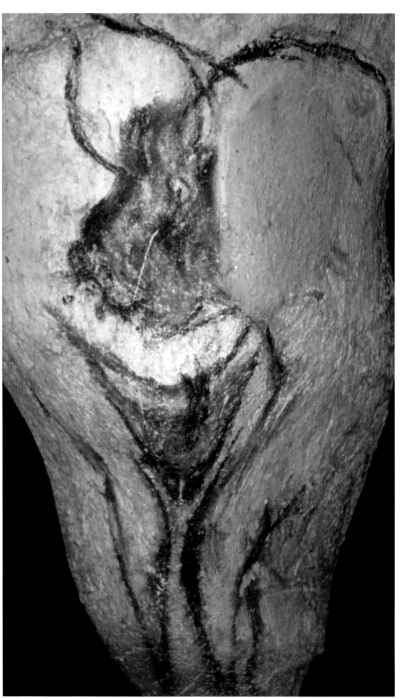

4

the "Venus of Hohle Fels", which is likely the oldest figurative depiction known and almost certainly the oldest representation of a human, points to the universal importance of human sexuality, reproduction and fertility in the world around us from the earliest beginnings of human artistic expression.

When considering the meaning of this figurine it is best to examine what is depicted and what is omitted. Given the difficulty of carving ivory, we can be sure that all aspects of an ivory carving were intended by its maker. The absence of a head shows that the woman is not a specific person but embodies attributes of being female in a more general sense. The absence of feet indicates that locomotion was not important for the understanding of the representation. Contrary to some claims, the Venus of Hohle Fels lacks the expanded lower abdomen of a pregnant woman. This being said, the highly visible vulva could be that of a woman just after giving birth. The depiction is both naked with the vulva and navel clearly visible, while at the same time lines resembling a kind of binding or clothing go all the way around the torso of the figurine. The figurine like many of the others from the Swabian Jura is also covered with numerous curved and geometric lines deeply incised into the carefully carved surface of the figurine. The breasts are full and project forward, together with the prominent vulva, making the sexual features the most outstanding positive characteristics of the figurine. The hands are depicted with great precision showing that the person or being depicted used her hands and had well developed tactile capabilities, perhaps of the kind needed to handle or breastfeed a new born infant. The ring carved directly into the ivory still shows signs of polish from being used to suspend the figurine, suggesting that the Venus was worn by a person or suspended from a cord.

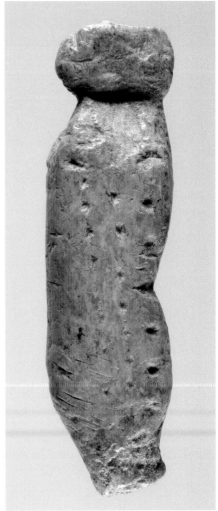

6 Geißenklösterle. Front-side of ivory platelet showing a therianthrope, H 3.8 cm   7 Hohle Fels. Lion Man, ivory, H 2.5 cm

While one can debate the specific meaning of the figurine, she is not a real person; instead she embodies concepts of fertility and reproduction. In human society this does not contradict the presence of an erotic aspect to the figurine. Still the figurine belongs more in the realm of female reproduction and midwifery than in the sphere of male eroticism. But also here, one perspective does not entirely contradict the other, and multiple meanings are inherent in all artistic master-pieces. Turning more to a biological model, we can be sure that the demographic success of a small group of Aurignacian hunters and gatherers in the Ach Valley hinged on the regular successful birth of healthy children by healthy mothers. Nothing would be more devastating to a newly arrived group of modern humans in the Upper Danube than the loss of woman of childbearing age. Finally, in a more general sense life in the Ice Age was only possible via a profound understanding of reproduction and an appreciation of fertility in world at large. Thus it is easy to image the Venus being meaningful both a specific human social context as well as in the harsh environmental contexts of the Swabian Ice Age in general. Here one only needs to imagine the joy and hope that would accompany the end of winters perhaps 15 degrees colder than today. The new vegetation of spring and the many animals it ultimately supported were essential for the survival and success of the Aurignacian people of the region, thus creating an explicit link between human social and economic life and human reproduction and fertility in general.

Nicholas J. Conard

With each passing year of new excavations in the caves of the Swabian Jura, more and more pieces of the puzzle of the region's Palaeolithic past come together. In this respect the excavations at Hohle Fels in 2002 were particularly noteworthy. While digging in the Aurignacian horizon IV, excavators recovered both the head of a waterbird and a small but remarkable carving of a Lion Man. This therianthropic depiction is only ca. 25 mm long and preserves only the left side of what was originally a larger figurine carved from mammoth ivory. The find is broken longitudinally along a natural bedding plane of the ivory, and the carving represents somewhat less than half of the original carving. Although the miniature Lion Man is modest in most respects, it would be hard to overestimate its importance. The find depicts a mixed human-animal image

bearing remarkable similarities to the original and much larger Lion Man from Hohlenstein-Stadel. The Lion Man from Hohle Fels is shown in a rigid, upright posture. Its composition and the parellel orientation of the legs, arms, torso and head are distinctly human while the ear and head resemble that of a lion or similar animal. The short arms and legs are reminiscent of the much more detailed carving of the Lion Man from Hohlenstein-Stadel as are the strong shoulder and neck.

This discovery, more than any other, documents that the Aurignacian archaeology of the Ach and Lone Valleys belong to the same cultural group in a strict sense. The finds demonstrate that the inhabitants of both valleys posessed a system of beliefs in which the transformation between human and animal played a central role. These images, along with the equally remarkable small depiction of a broadly similar therianthrope from archaeological horizon II at Geißenklösterle correspond to three figurative artworks showing a mythical entity that we can characterize as a Lion Man. When one considers how unlikely it would be to even find one such figurine, the discovery of three similar depictions in the very small areas of the caves that have been excavated must indicate that these depictions were a significant part of the system of beliefs of the Aurignacian people of the Swabian Jura.

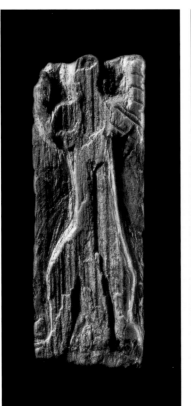

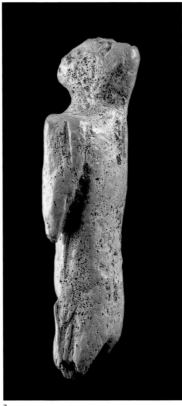

6

7

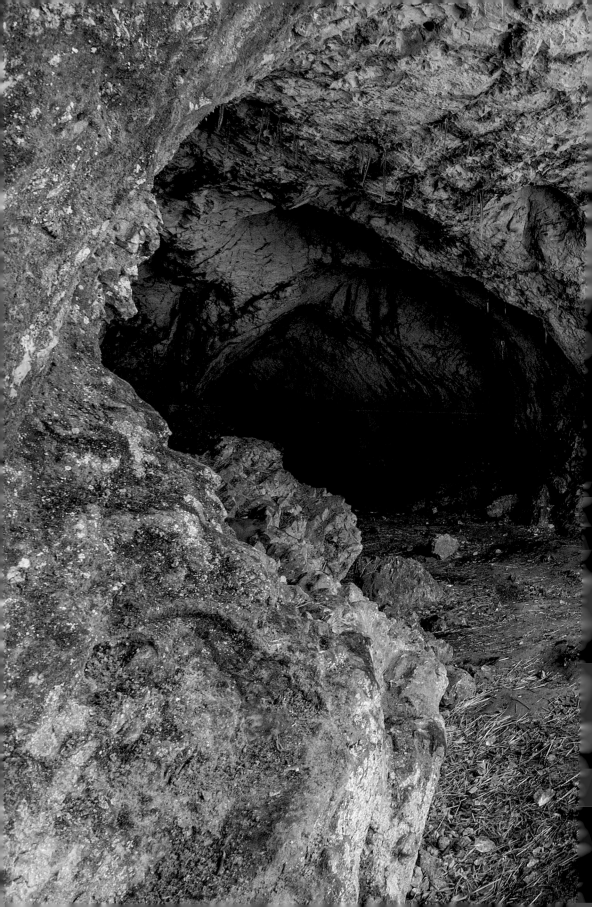

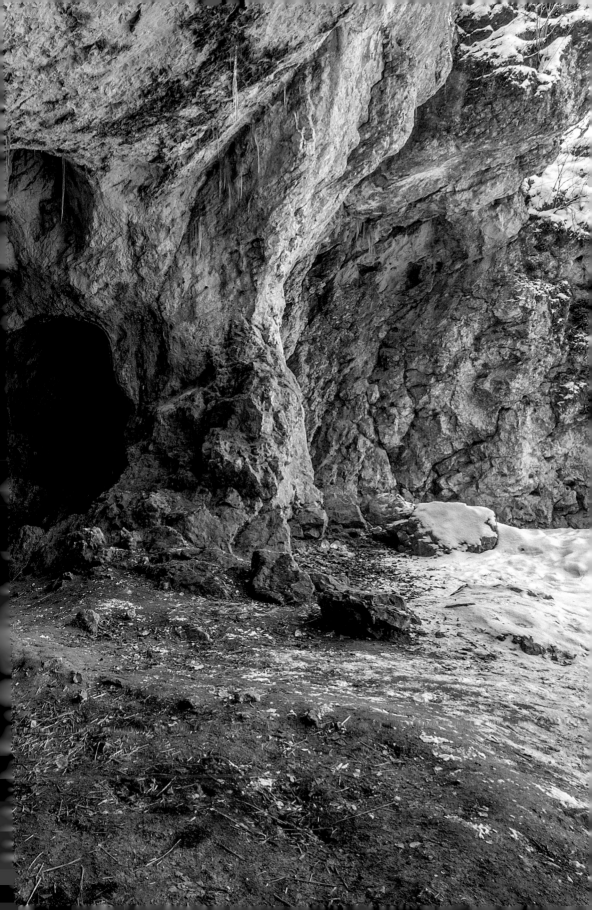

BETWEEN ANIMAL AND MAN

FANTASTIC CREATURES IN THE ART OF THE ICE AGE
KURT WEHRBERGER

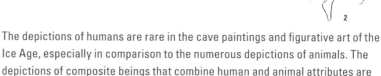

2

The depictions of humans are rare in the cave paintings and figurative art of the Ice Age, especially in comparison to the numerous depictions of animals. The depictions of composite beings that combine human and animal attributes are even more scarce. Cave paintings of animal-man hybrids were only found in a handful of caves, including, for example, the caves from the south of France: Le Gabillou (Dordogne), Les Trois Frères (Ariège) and Chauvet Pont-d'Arc (Rhône-Alpes). In all cases, the head and upper body of an animal was placed on a human lower body. Reversed combinations are not known.

The coupling of human attributes with those of a bison was found multiple times, e.g. in the combination with the lower extremities of a woman from Chauvet, the "L'homme-bison" from Le Gabillou or the two scratched figures from Les Trois Frères. One of these seems to be carrying a curved object that is often interpreted as a musical instrument. Probably the most well-known animal-human hybrid figure, the "magician/

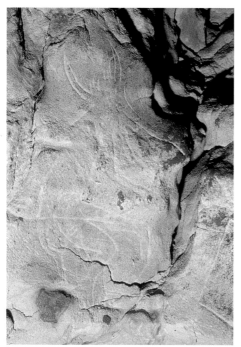

1

sorcier" or "horned god/dieu cornu" was also found in Les Trois Frères. It is the only figure in the cave that was partially scratched and partially painted onto the wall. The body is depicted from the side, the head from the front. The head has large, bird-like eyes, reindeer or bison-like ears, a long pointed beard and antlers. The broad upper body with the curved tail reminds us of a horse while the upper extremities look like the paws of a bear or a big cat. The legs and feet are human. The genitals indicate that this mix of animal and man is clearly male. These com-

posite beings are always shown with bent legs and convey the impression of a body in motion. The placement of these animal-human hybrids in the caves is worth mentioning. They were almost always found in the remote corners of the cave, apart from the large animal murals. This is the case for the "L'homme-bison", which is located at the farthest end of the very narrow and low Le Gabillou cave. In Chauvet Pont-d'Arc, the bison-woman figure is also located in the most remote corridor of the cave near the large lion panorama. In Les Trois Frères, the composite being is located at 3.5 meter height and looks down upon the visitors at the end of a small side corridor. The described animal-human hybrid wall art is assigned to the later periods of the Upper Paleolithic. The so far oldest depiction of a composite being is the Paleolithic painting found during recent excavations at the Fumane cave in the Lessinian Mountains near Verona in Northern Italy. Multiple red paintings on pieces of limestone, including a horned figure with human posture, were found in the 35,000 year old layers.

1, 2 Le Gabillou. L'homme-bison, engraving on cave wall, H 37 cm
3, 4 Les Trois Frères. Magician (sorcier) or horned god (dieu cornu). Painting and engraving on cave ceiling, L 75 cm

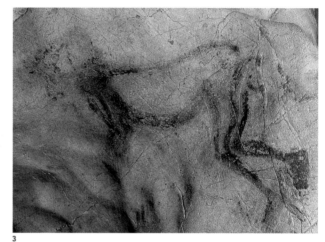

3

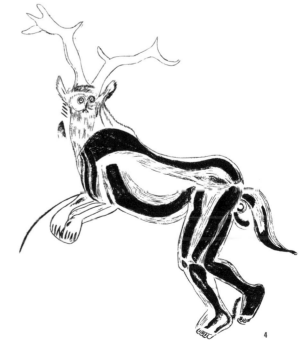

4

5 Fumane. Magician (sciamano), Painting on limestone, H 24 cm   **6** Les Trois Frères. L'homme-bison, Engraving on cave wall, H 30 cm   **7** Shaman of the Siberian Tungus. Sketch by the Dutch traveler Nicolas Witsen from the early 18th century

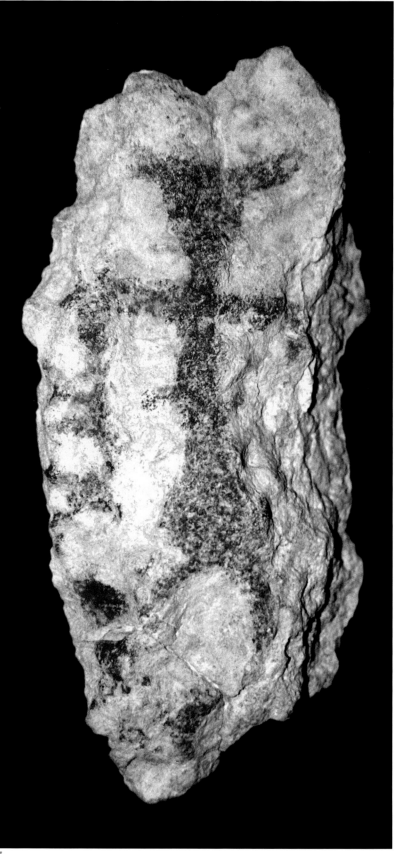

Three-dimensional representations of composite beings from the start of the Upper
Paleolithic are so far limited to sites in Southwestern Germany. The statuette of the
Lion Man was identified as an animal-man hybrid soon after it was first fit together.
It was soon joined by the smaller presumed Lion Man sculpture from the Hohle Fels.
The figure on the ivory platelet from the Geißenklösterle cave may also be a mixed
being. It has also been suggested that it could be interpreted as a miniature Lion
Man.

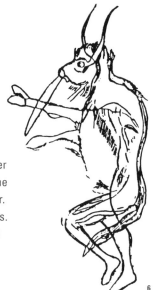

6

<u>Excursus</u> **Schamanism**
Kurt Wehrberger

The complex, religio-social phenomenon shamanism was originally
only applied to Siberia and Northern Asia. It is primarily characteristic for hunter-gatherer societies whose conception of the world
mirrors their daily interaction with nature. Shamanism is based on
the belief that animals and humans exist as equal partners and can
communicate with one another. The world is populated by spirits
or gods that can adopt anthropomorphic or animalistic features.
Shamen can have multiple functions and can act as fortunetellers,
priests and healers.

Throughout the course of a shamanistic session, the shaman experiences several different stages of consciousness – sometimes
enhanced by intoxicating substances. At the start of the trance, the
shaman sees geometric patterns such as
zigzag lines, dots, meanders etc. In a
second phase, he tries to interpret these
forms as specific, known objects. The
third phase of the trance is a kind of
vortex or tunnel that leads to a world of
hallucinations. In this world, the shaman
believes he can fly or he can assume the
role of an animal, either partially or
completely. Neuropsychological research
has shown that these phases are common to everyone and are contingent upon
the nervous system. Only the hallucino-
genic third phase is culture specific,
you only see – even if it may be altered
from reality – things that you have seen
or experienced in real life.

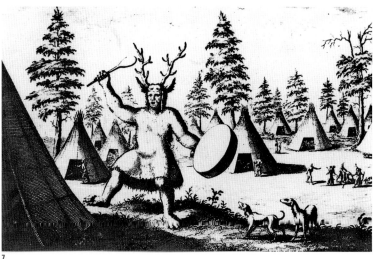

7

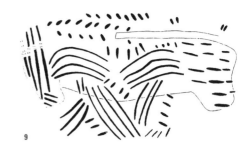

9

The animal-human hybrids are fantasy figures that cannot be analyzed with logic.
Sometimes it is difficult to determine which features are human and which features are animal. What was the idea behind these compositions? Are these composite beings fictional, abstract figures from the imagination of Ice Ages societies,
do they represent gods? It seems too simple to associate people wrapped in animal skins and wearing animal masks with hunting rituals. It seems more plausible
that the beings represent Shaman, people with extraordinary spiritual capabilities
who were able to broaden their consciousness and communicate with the world
of spirits. Ethnological studies have shown that shamanistic rituals often included
costumes and masks.

Shamanistic practices have also been assumed for the human societies of the
Upper Paleolithic that created the cave paintings and three-dimensional figurines.
These depictions do not necessarily have to be the result of such practices. They
may have been accessories of shamanistic practices as is assumed for the smaller
figurines. Or they were created to provide evidence of these phenomena, as part
of a visual story like the paintings and engravings in the caves.

Although there is a significant difference in age, multiple millennia, the animal-
human hybrids among the cave paintings are important for the interpretation
of the composite beings among the figurines from the Aurignacian of the Swabian
Jura. The parallels in the combination of features are remarkable in respect of

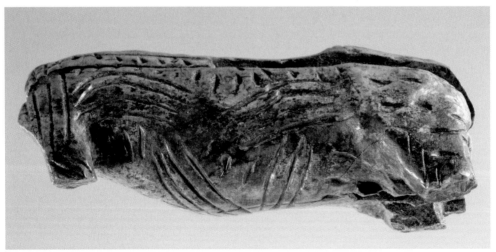

8

the Lion Man figure: The head and upper body of one or more animals on top of human legs and feet. Another aspect is movement: The bent posture of the composite beings among the cave painting can be interpreted as a dancing posture. The figure on the ivory platelet from the Geißenklösterle cave also looks like it is in motion. The composite being has both arms raised. Its legs look like they are moving; the right leg is bent more than the left leg. Although the Lion Man figure seems to have been created in a static posture, this is more likely a result of the nature of the material. It seems that the artist tried to include motion in the figure: The soles of the feet were not placed horizontally in a resting position; they were carved at a slight angle, which suggests tension in the body and may imply that the figure was getting ready to jump.

Finally, almost all of the three-dimensional figurines were also covered with carved symbols such as notches, lines, crosses or dots. Their interpretation as simple decorative elements seems unlikely; it is possible that these symbols, which were primarily applied to the body axis and the extremities, correspond to the geometric patterns that are counted among the hallucinations one sees during shamanistic rituals. The parallels of the decorations on the Lion Man from the Hohlenstein Stadel and the composite being from the Geißenklösterle are especially interesting: One arm of the statue was marked with a row of horizontal notches. Similar notches were also applied to both arms of the flat relief. The sequence of notches and dots on the narrow edge and the back of the ivory platelet were also cause for fantastic speculations about the symbolism of numbers.

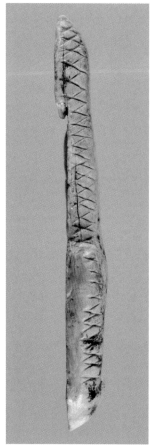

11

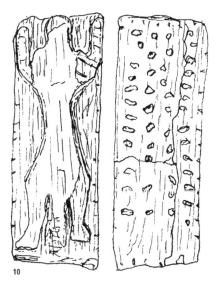

10

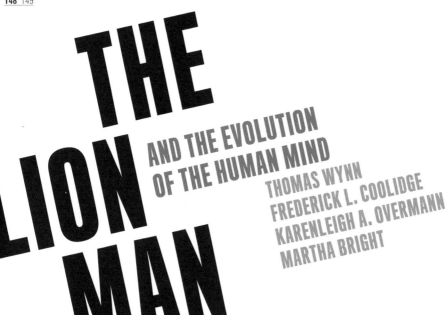

THE LION MAN

AND THE EVOLUTION OF THE HUMAN MIND

THOMAS WYNN
FREDERICK L. COOLIDGE
KARENLEIGH A. OVERMANN
MARTHA BRIGHT

Unlike the animals depicted in cave paintings, no one ever actually saw a Lion Man. No lion-human hybrids inhabited Ice Age Europe, and thus the Lion Man represents an unambiguous work of imagination. A product of the imagination of this type was something new in the behavioral repertoire of our human ancestors, and it indicates that their minds were very like our own.

The Lion Man reveals several interesting things about the mind that imagined it. First, the prehistoric artisan relied on well-defined concepts of 'lion' and 'human'. Modern people think about natural phenomena by using what cognitive anthropologists term 'folk biology', a process of categorization with two organizing principles. The first is "essentialism": Every natural category is defined by inherent qualities possessed by members of the category. The category 'lions' is defined by qualities such as color, strength, and ferocity. Second, categories are organized into hierarchies of more inclusive categories. So, lions are also 'cats', and cats are 'animals', with those higher-order categories being more abstract. All people, no matter what their language or culture, categorize in this way, so 'folk biology' is almost certainly an inherent feature of human cognition, and cognitive scientists have identified parts of the brain that support it: the temporal lobes (low on the sides of the brain) for essentialism, the parietal lobes (high on the sides and the top) for hierarchism. One of the interesting things about folk categories is that they need not be the result of an actual, waking perceptual experience; the natural world is not actually

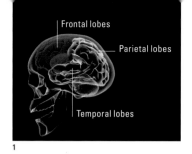

1

divided up into such nice, neat packages. Instead, brains impose this order on a chaotic world of variability, whether we are awake or asleep. Folk biology likely evolved long ago, perhaps with Homo erectus, and it was almost certainly a component of Neandertal cognition. The artisan who imagined the Lion Man would have drawn upon folk-biology categories because 'lion' and 'human' are so distinct.

The cognitive system for folk biology is not, however, what made the artisan's imagination so new and different. The artisan also had the cognitive ability for abstraction, which rests on two kinds of thinking, analysis and synthesis. Analysis decomposed the concepts of 'lion' and 'human' to extract their essential elements, while synthesis recombined selected elements to create a concept of something that did not exist in the physical world. The ability to analyze and synthesize conceptual elements, as the artisan did to create the Lion Man, required another cognitive process called "working memory". Working memory is the ability to hold and manipulate information 'in the mind', as in mentally adding up a list of numbers or thinking through a problem to be solved. Working memory is largely a function of the frontal lobes (located high toward the front of the brain, behind the forehead), the seat of the executive functions responsible for cognitive functions such as reasoning, problem solving, and attention, as well as the parietal lobes, which not only integrate information from the senses but also perform complex association processes, including higher-level cross-domain thinking such as that involved in metaphor. Further, the parietal lobes appeared to have expanded in Homo sapiens but not in Neandertals, perhaps, one of the key neurological differences between the two human types. The cognitive processing implied by the Lion Man suggests that the artisan had a greater working memory capacity than his or her ancestors did, an enhancement that was one of the key evolutionary acquisitions in human cognition. As we have hinted, it is also possible that the idea of a Lion Man first came together in a dream or a trance. One effect of hallucinogens is the same conceptual taking apart and recombining. But it is unlikely that the brain would do this, even in a trance state, if it did not possess this ability in real time. Interestingly, therianthropes (half-person, half-beast) are not uncommon dream characters, particularly in children. Thus, the Lion Man, in all likelihood, represents the thinking processes of a fully modern mind, possibly one that came about as a result of a dream – for why should radically new ideas be restricted to waking consciousness?

1 The frontal lobes support working memory and other executive functions. The parietal lobes support hierarchism in categorization, sensory integration, and higher-level associations, such as metaphor; they are expanded in Homo sapiens but not in Neandertals. The temporal lobes support essentialism in categorization

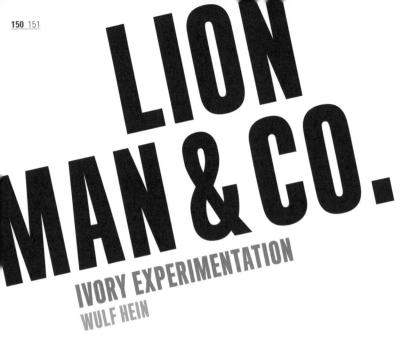

LION MAN & CO.

IVORY EXPERIMENTATION
WULF HEIN

Mammoth tusks were special among the raw materials available to Paleolithic humans. Flint stone, antler, wood and bone were primarily used for the production of common objects necessary for daily life while the "white gold" was almost exclusively reserved for the fabrication of jewelry and art.

As an archeological technician I am primarily interested in the characteristics of the raw material instead of the interpretation and function of the objects:

Which raw materials were chosen?
How well can they be manipulated and processed using the typical tools from that period?
How long did the working process take?
How do the characteristics of the material and the tools influence the form of the objects?
Is it possible to influence the ivory in some way to simplify the working process?

In order to find answers to these questions, I have reproduced numerous finds from the Aurignacian layers from the caves in the Ach and Lone Valleys, including beads, small statuettes, such as the horse from the Vogelherd, the Venus from the Hohle Fels, and the Lion Man from the Hohlenstein-Stadel.

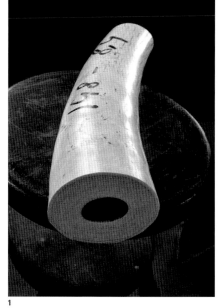

1

In 2009, the Ulmer Museum commissioned a replica of the Lion Man statue that was to be made using authentic tools and techniques from the Paleolithic. Due to financial concerns it was not possible to acquire a piece of mammoth ivory for this project; however, we were able to procure a piece of legally imported elephant ivory that largely met our requirements. The Paleolithic artist chose his piece of ivory in such a way that the pulpa (the cone shaped opening for nerves on the inside of the tusk) ended in the crotch of the figure so that he did not have to spend a lot of time and energy preparing the space between the legs of the statue. The natural form of the raw materials obviously played a key role in the selection of the material for numerous other objects as well. The blanks were not carved from a larger piece of ivory. Instead, fitting pieces were searched out and selected; in the case of the animal statuettes, these pieces were often split pieces recognizable by to their slightly curved cross-section. Recent evidence also suggests that older ivory was also collected and worked – a fish hook from the site Wustermark was fashioned out of a piece of mammoth tusk that is ca. 9,000 years older than the site itself.

It is not possible to safely say whether the Lion Man was carved from an older, heavily weathered tusk fragment that had the general shape of the planned object or whether it was an object trouvée whose form may have inspired the artist to create the composite creature. The preserved details and the surface structure of the figure lead me to believe that the statue was carved out of the entire tip of a mammoth tusk. During the production of the replica, I tested different techniques and used numerous flint tools typical for the Aurignacian period.

1 Raw material for the ivory whittler: A 3.8 kg elephant tusk fragment with pulp cavity

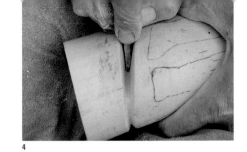

4

CUT TO LENGTH

of a tusk is either possible via hard percussion using a hammer stone, this works relatively well if the tusk is frozen (private communication Sibylle Wolf), or by making a circular notch around the tusk. By means of this technique, a notch is first "sawed" around the surface of the tooth using a flint blade and then broadened using a burin until the pulp cavity is reached.

CARVING

as in removing large shavings, was not possible. Large flint blades that could be used as chisels did not withstand the pressure and quickly broke apart.

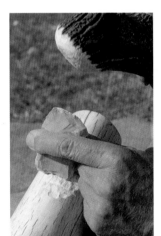

SCRAPING

was the only method that allowed me to remove larger amounts of material from the fresh, hard ivory in a controlled fashion. It resulted in concave forms.

RASPING

was possible using the rough edge of any stone tool, however, the method was not very efficient because the working edges quickly became dull.

GRINDING OR POLISHING

was not necessary because it was possible to easily smooth the surface using the edge of a burin.

2

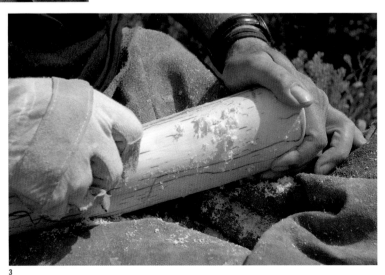

3

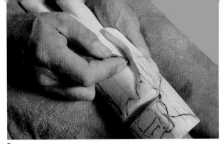
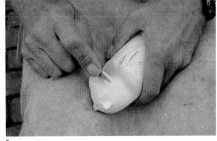

5   6

2–6 A work in progress: The formation of a new Lion Man

The majority of the work on the figure was carried out by scraping using a burin and other suitable flakes: It was strenuous and tiring work, especially when larger amounts of material needed to be removed. The process of carving the details was, in contrast, relaxing and educational. In sum, I invested over 360 working hours into the reproduction of the figure; this number can only be an approximation of the total amount of work necessary for the actual production. For example, I have documented the reproduction of the horse figurine from the Vogelherd three times; the required hours of work were 35, 32 and 30 hours respectively.

Generally, tools made out of flint can be used to make any imaginable form out of ivory; however, indentions and undercuts are very difficult to form, especially when working against the grain of the material. It was very difficult and time consuming to fashion the arms of the statue, therefore it does not seem likely that they were completely separated from the statue. In addition to the significant extra work, the arms would be very fragile if they are not attached to the body at some point.

While working on the tusk, the material was repeatedly soaked in water – this softened the outer layer, alleviated the work and spared the tools. Soaking the material for a longer period of time did not improve it any further, however, soaking the ivory in oxalic acid softened the material and then allowed it to harden and become stabile again. Whether this process was applied to a figure of this size is questionable – the necessary plants (common sorrel) would have been available in the Paleolithic. During a workshop on the topic of ivory carving, I was able to observe the impact of soaking pieces of elephant ivory that originated from different areas of the same tusk: Some pieces did not change at all, others swelled with water, were then easily carved and finally hardened again.

No matter from what "cloth" the Lion Man was cut – one thing is certain:
He was not made over the course of a weekend.

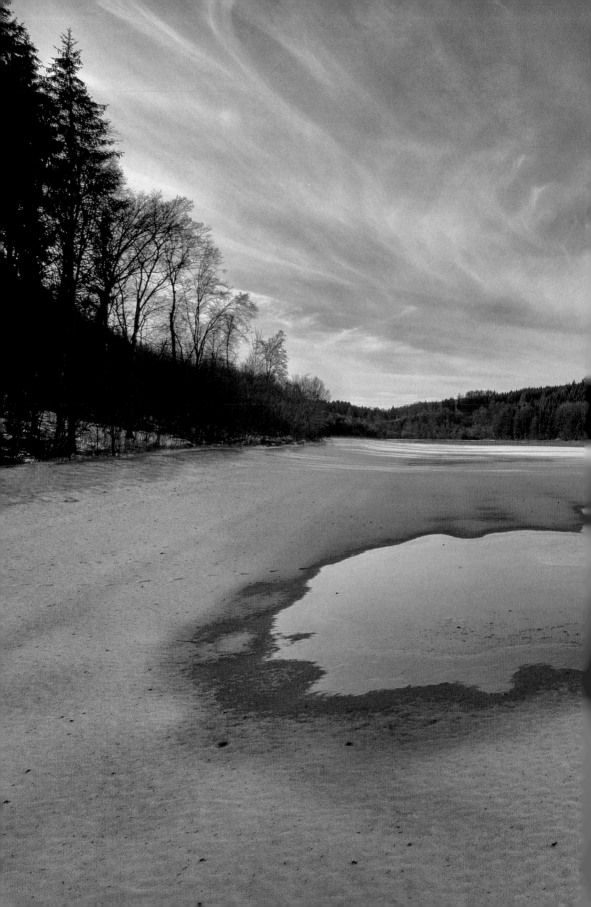

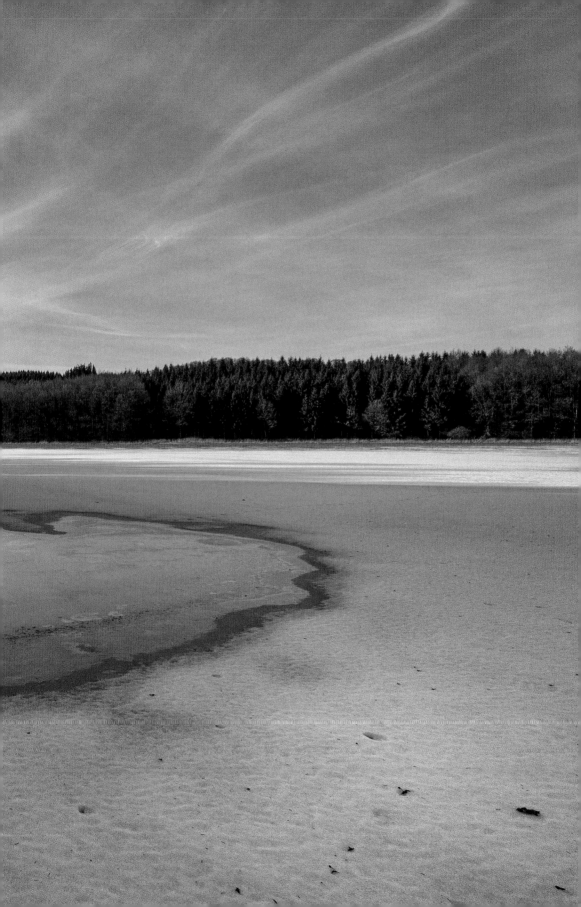

DEPOT – HIDING PLACE – CULT SITE?

THE CHAMBER OF THE LION MAN

CLAUS-JOACHIM KIND
KURT WEHRBERGER

1 Reindeer antler fragments from the chamber of the Lion Man   **2** The chamber of the Lion Man during the 2012 excavation

The spectrum of finds from the back of the Stadel cave shows that the cave must have been used differently than the "regular" settlement sites in the Vogelherd, the Geißenklösterle or the Hohle Fels from the start of the Upper Paleolithic (Aurignacian). Figurative ivory art was found at all four sites; however, their places of discovery in the caves vary. While the objects of art in these three caves were found together with usual settlement debris among hundreds of faunal bones and stone tools, the Lion Man in the Stadel cave was discovered on the periphery of the settlement area in an exposed location. Very few remains of human activities, with the exception of some pieces of jewelry, were found in the area around the find place of the statuette although the sediments were carefully excavated and sieved. These include pendants made out of ivory and perforated teeth from red deer, fox and wolf.

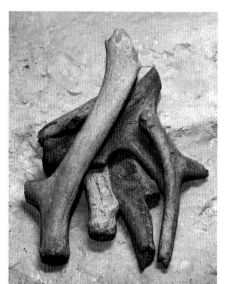

1

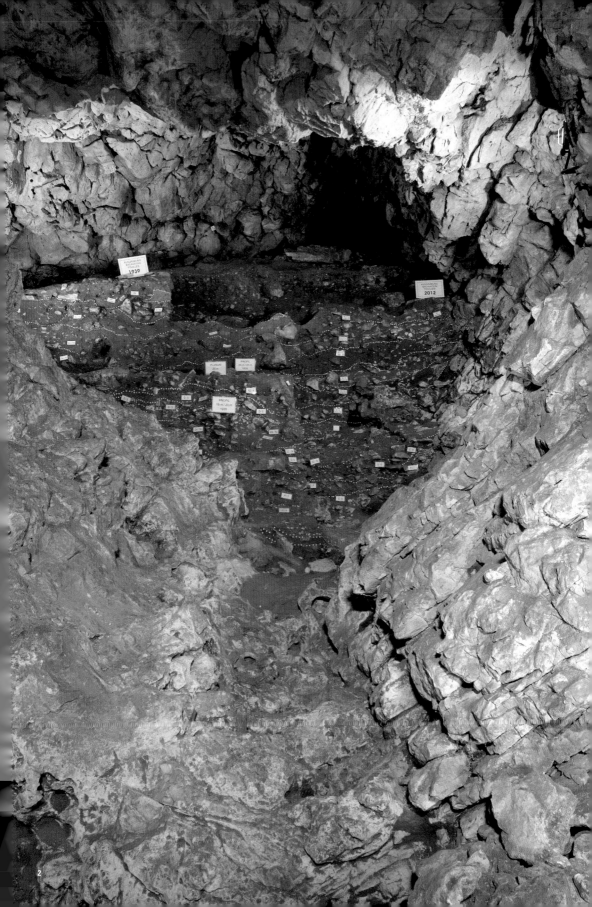

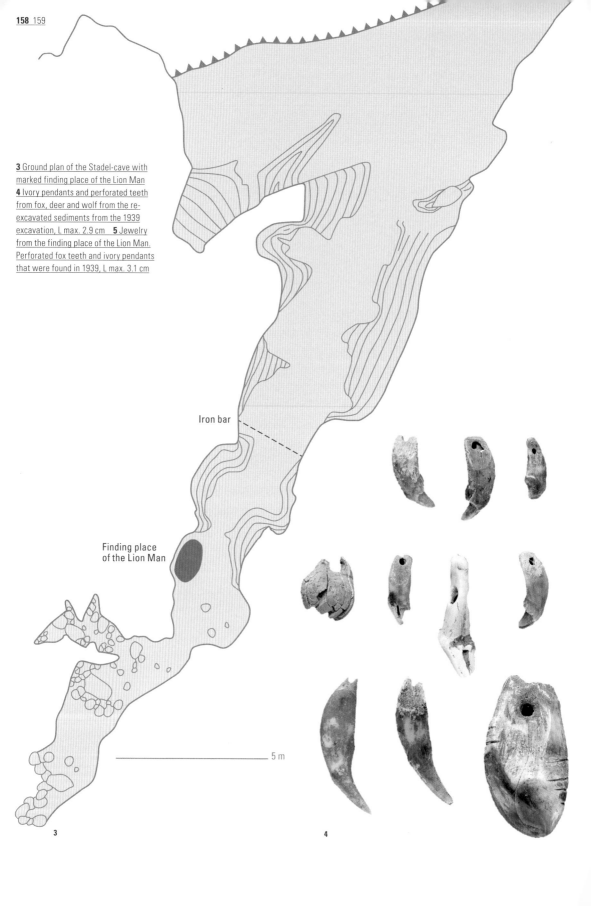

3 Ground plan of the Stadel-cave with marked finding place of the Lion Man
4 Ivory pendants and perforated teeth from fox, deer and wolf from the re-excavated sediments from the 1939 excavation, L max. 2.9 cm   **5** Jewelry from the finding place of the Lion Man. Perforated fox teeth and ivory pendants that were found in 1939, L max. 3.1 cm

Iron bar

Finding place
of the Lion Man

5 m

3

4

Objects made out of bone and antler are relatively frequent in the Aurignacian layers, especially compared to the smaller number of stone artifacts. They include a 50 cm long smoother made from a split mammoth rib, one of the few completely preserves specimens of this tool type, which may have been used to process skins and pelts. The concentration of antler fragments from reindeer inside the cave is also noteworthy. An analysis of the faunal remains from the 1939 excavation by Keiko Kitagawa from the University of Tübingen showed that smaller and larger fragments of relatively thin shed antlers and antler points were present in all of the Paleolithic layers. However, hundreds of fragments were found in the Aurignacian horizons, especially in the back of the cave. This is an extraordinarily higher number of fragments compared to the Middle Paleolithic and later Upper Paleolithic (Magdalenian) layers. At the risk of over-interpreting these results, there are parallels to similar unusual concentrations of antlers in other Paleolithic cave sites in Eurasia that have been interpreted as ritual deposition.

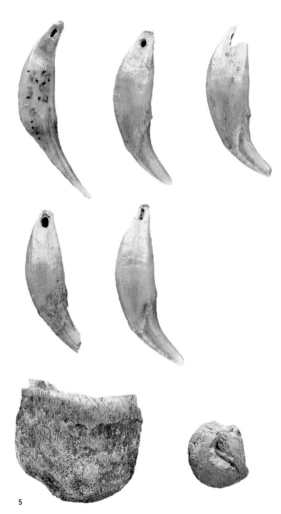

Evidence suggests that the finding place of the Lion Man, the small chamber in the back of the cave, was a special one. The figure was obviously deposited together with pieces of jewelry at a location far inside the cave that was set apart from the work and living spaces. Maybe it was a hiding place and the statuette and the other objects were never recovered. Maybe it was a location reserved for cultic, totemic or shamanistic rituals with the mysterious Lion Man at their center.

6 Hohlenstein-Stadel. Jawbone from a cave lion in situ, L 27 cm **7** Hohlenstein-Stadel. Mammoth tusks 1939, L max. 17 cm **8** Hohlenstein-Stadel. Mammoth tusk 1960. 3D simulation of a part of the tusk after the computer-tomography scan **9** Hohlenstein-Stadel. Mammoth tusk during its excavation 1960

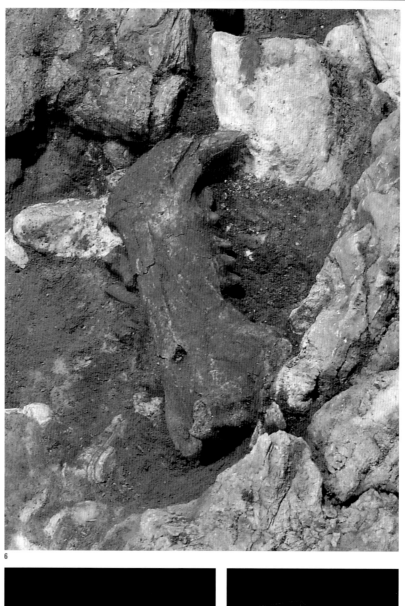

6

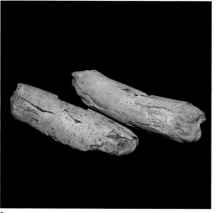

7

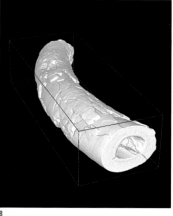

8

Excursus **Mammoth teeth and lion jaw**
Claus Joachim Kind, Kurt Wehrberger, Sibylle Wolf

The back of the Stadel cave was already used as a place to store special objects before the time of the Lion Man. During the 1939 and 1960 excavations, an accumulation of ivory was found in the deeper layers from the time of the Neanderthals in a small area near and inside the chamber in which the statuette was found. Two mammoth tusks from the 1939 excavation are especially remarkable. Both are about 17 cm long and show traces of being worked – they are chisel-like on both ends. In the chamber in front of the "Lion Man's chamber", separated by a ridge of stone from the rest of the cave, excavators during the 1960 excavation found a ca. 50 cm long, nearly completely preserved mammoth tusk.

The end of the tusk closest to the head shows evidence of tools used to detach the tusk from the skull, the pulp cavity continues into the tooth for almost 20 cm. The distal end of the tooth shows wear and tear through regular use by the mammoth while collecting food. All three tusks also bear tooth marks and evidence of having been chewed on both ends by carnivores, probably by cave hyenas. However, it is not plausible that hyenas dragged the teeth into the cave. It is more likely that young animals of the pack used the back of the Stadel cave as their den and gnawed on the tusks that had been left behind in the chamber. They quickly left off of the tusks because ivory is not very nourishing. The 20 cm long right lower jawbone of a cave lion was found during the 2012 excavation. It was wedged between two pieces of rock in the Middle Paleolithic layer K. The excavators also recovered an accumulation of charcoal, burned bones and limestone with burn marks on them from this area. They are evidence that Neanderthals, whose temporary presence in the Stadel cave is documented for the area near the entrance of the cave, must have also occupied this relatively dark back portion of the cave.

THE LION MAN AND THE MEDIA LANDSCAPE

A LONG ROAD TO WORLDWIDE FAME

WOLF-HENNING PETERSHAGEN

The ivory figure from the Stadel cave in the Lone Valley was first presented to the wide-eyed public on March 16th, 1970 at the opening of the Prehistoric Collections (Prähistorische Sammlungen) in Ulm. This was its first public appearance after 35,000 years. The numerous fragments of the statuette were originally found on August 25th, 1939. Yet they were not reassembled until more than three decades later, just a few months prior to their presentation at the opening of the exhibition. Although it was still a mystery what exactly the figure was meant to represent, it was a perfect sensation. The national press reported about the "probably oldest artistic depiction made by mankind" (Augsburger Zeitung, March 19th, 1970).

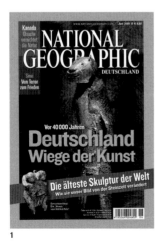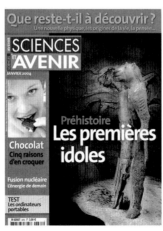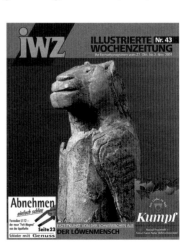

1

On March 27th, 1970, the journal "Die ZEIT" spread the word about the "Animal-Man Hybrid from Ulm" throughout all of Germany. Afterwards, aside from some contributions in international professional journals, it grew quiet concerning the statuette. In the following years, additional fragments were found. These helped to complete the face of the figure – the face of a lion! Initially, only members, customers or business acquaintances of the Ulmer Volksbank were fortunate enough to see and hear about this very adventurous tale of discovery and reconstruction: It was included as episode 17 in the series "Ulmer Stadtgeschichte" as part of the bank's annual report in May 1983.

The public again became aware of the figurine in 1988 when it was professionally restored for the first time. Interestingly, the question of the statuette's gender predominated the discussion. It had previously been addressed as male, after the restoration it was assumed to be female. The discussion was nearly ideological and captured the attention of the media. In the end, the discussion was a dead end because all evidence for one side or the other was at best speculative, not factual. In the first large special exhibition on the subject, the Ulmer Museum decided on the designation "Löwenmensch – Lion Man" ("man" as in mankind). This name represents the figurine from the Stadel cave in numerous languages worldwide.

1 Title-pages of the journals "National Geographic" from June 2009, „Sciences et avenir" from January 2004 and IWZ (Illustrierte Wochenzeitung) from Nov. 10th, 2001 **2** Overview of the exhibition "Den kennt doch keiner! Löwenmensch und Medienwelt" in the Studio Archäologie of the Ulmer Museum (2013/14)

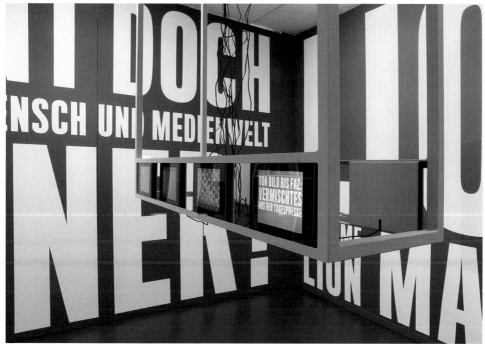

The international fame of the ivory figure grew slowly but steadily from this point on. In Germany, popular science journals such as GEO, P.M., "Archäologie In Deutschland" and "Bild der Wissenschaft" printed archeological and historical articles about the Lion Man. In connection with other disciplines, articles about the figure were also published in journals such as "Gehirn & Geist". Authors from the "Stern" or "Der Spiegel" wrote about the statuette numerous times, journals such as "La Recherche" or "Sciences et avenir" added to its popularity in France. In the United States of America, the magazine of the "National Geographic Society" helped spread the figure's fame throughout Europe, America and Asia. Popular articles in numerous customer magazines spread the news of the statuette to their readers and introduced them to the Lion Man.

In the world of books, the statuette was at first only mentioned in archeological books or exhibition catalogues. The spectrum quickly expanded to works of history and art history, biology and evolutionary research, religious studies and psychology. Aside from the German literature, English and French literature predominates. These primarily include compendiums, encyclopedias, standard texts and monographs. In recent years, the fame of the Lion Man has spread farther east, as evidenced by Japanese publications on the subject. The figure is also an advertising star and figures in a series of travel guides and regional

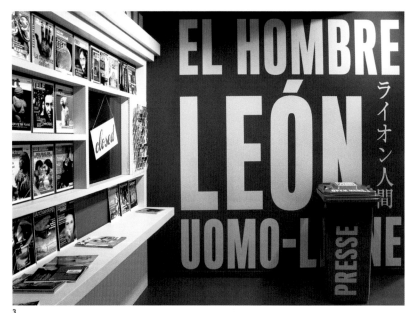

literature on southern Germany, specifically on the Swabian Jura. First attempts to incorporate him into novels include children's and young adult literature. Its longest voyage was the journey of the Lion Man into school books in the year 2000. Since then, the Lion Man has found its way into

3

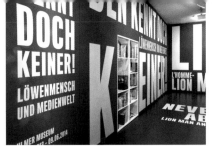

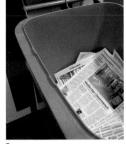

4   5

the teaching materials in Baden-Württemberg and other German states as well as into the teaching materials in France, the homeland of prehistoric archeology. In the United States, the Lion Man is discussed in college textbooks. Placed back to back the books in which the Lion Man is mentioned have a length of nearly five meters – that does not include magazines and journals. The Lion Man is also a film star and appears primarily in documentaries. These range from scientific programs such as Planet Wissen (SWR) or Quarks & Co. (WDR) to German documentations such as "Terra X" (ZDF) and international programs such as the BBC. A figure that re-sembled the Lion Man had a slightly curious appearance in a scene of the film by Werner Herzog "The cave of forgotten dreams (Die Höhle der vergessenen Träume)" (2012) about the Grotte Chauvet. A French archeologist presented a Lion Man that looked as though it had been fashioned as a puppet for the Augs-burger Puppenkiste. In 2005, the popularity of the Lion Man was so great that the "Innovationsregion Ulm" included him in their nation-wide promotion of the region. In the newspaper "Die ZEIT", the region placed a full-paged advertisement together with the state of Baden-Württemberg: A sketch of the family tree of prominent citizens of Ulm with the Lion Man at its roots.

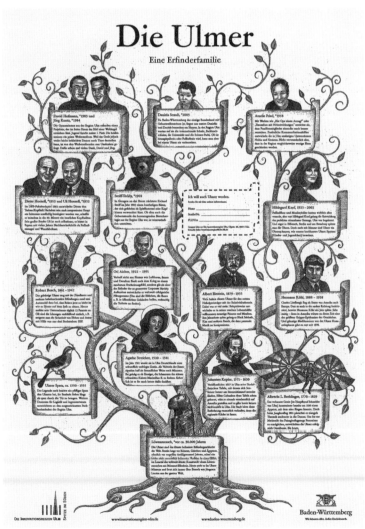

6

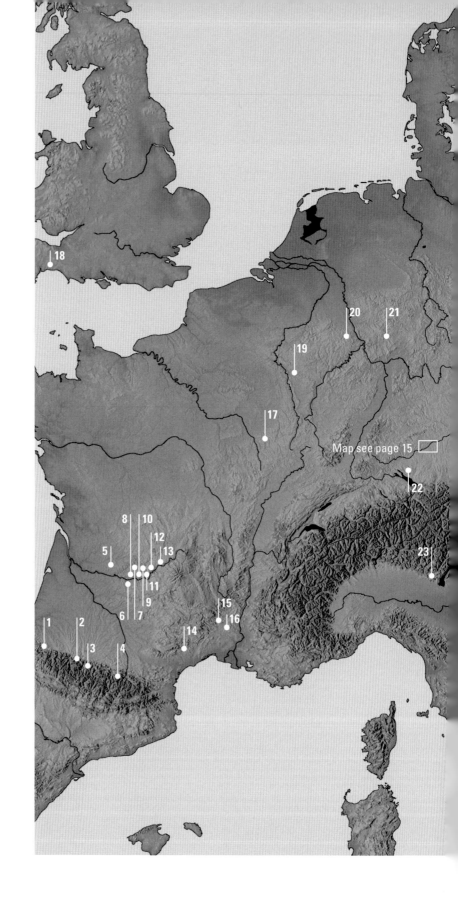

**European Paleolithic sites
mentioned in the book**

France
1 Isturitz
2 Aurignac
3 Les Trois Frères
4 La Vache
5 La Quina-Aval
6 La Gravette
7 La Madeleine
8 Le Gabillou
9 Rouffignac
10 Cellier
11 La Ferrasie
12 Blanchard
13 Castanet
14 Aldène
15 Chauvet-Pont-d'Arc
16 La Baume Latrone
17 Arcy-sur-Cure

England
18 Kent's Cavern

Belgium
19 Trou Magrite

Germany
20 Lommersum
21 Wildscheuer
22 Schussenquelle

Italy
23 Fumane
24 Cavallo

Austria
25 Stratzing/Krems-Rehberg
26 Willendorf

Czech Republic
27 Dolní Věstonice
28 Pavlov

Romania
29 Peștera cu Oase
30 Coliboia

Map see page 15

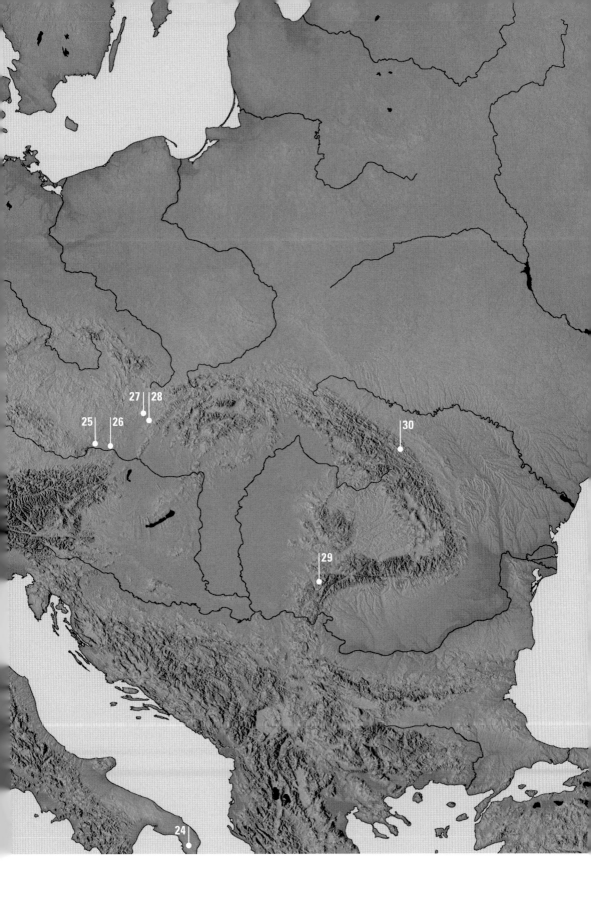

We would like to thank all of our authors and lenders for their support, especially all colleagues from different institutions as well as private persons and friends, who accompanied and supported our projects concerning the Lion Man in different ways in past and present.

Urgeschichtliches Museum (Blaubeuren)
Georg Hiller, Dr. Stephanie Kölbl,
Johannes Wiedmann M.A.

Landesamt für Denkmalpflege im Regierungs-
präsidium Stuttgart (Esslingen)
Thomas Beutelspacher M.A., Dr. Jörg Bofinger,
Dipl.-Restauratorin Nicole Ebinger-Rist,
Prof. Dr. Claus-Joachim Kind, Prof. Dr. Dirk
Krausse, Anette Lerch, Yvonne Mühleis,
Prof. Dr. Claus Wolf

Archäologisches Landesmuseum
Baden-Württemberg (Konstanz, Rastatt)
Dr. Jörg Heiligmann, Patricia Schlemper M.A.

Soprintendente per i beni archeologici
del Veneto (Padova, Italy)
Dr. Marianna Bressan, Dr. Vincenzo Tiné

Naturkunde- und Mammutmuseum (Siegsdorf)
Dr. Robert Darga

Landesmuseum Württemberg (Stuttgart)
Prof. Dr. Cornelia von Ewigleben,
Dr. Erwin Keefer

Staatliches Museum für Naturkunde/
Museum am Löwentor (Stuttgart)
Thomas Rathgeber, Dr. Reinhard Ziegler

Universität Tübingen
Prof. Dr. Michael Bolus, Judy-yun Chang M.A.,
Prof. Nicholas J. Conard Ph.D., Prof. Dr. Bernd
Engler, Prof. Dr. Harald Floss, Hilde Jensen,
Keiko Kitagawa M.A., Prof. Dr. Johannes
Krause, Maria Malina, Dr. Susanne C. Münzel,
Prof. Dr. Ernst Seidl, Sibylle Wolf M.A.,
Mohsen Zeidi M.A.

Naturhistorisches Museum (Vienna, Austria)
Dr. Walpurga Antl-Weiser, Dr. Anton Kern

Braun Engels Gestaltung (Ulm)
Gerhard Braun, Marietta Fischer, Birgit Lupia,
Sabine Lutz, Kerstin Öchsler

Dr. Joachim Bayer (Langenau); Prof. Dr.-Ing. Uwe
Berger (Hochschule Technik und Wirtschaft,
Aalen); Armin Bollinger (Asselfingen); Jill Cook
(Britisches Museum, London, England); Christina
von Elm M.A. – Die Zeichnerei (Tübingen); Frank
Findeiß – echtzeitmedia (Güntersleben); Wulf
Hein (Dorn-Assenheim); Uwe Krüger – spelefilm
(Rammingen); Dr. Christine Neugebauer-Maresch
(Österreichische Akademie der Wissenschaften,
Wien, Österreich); Astrid Preuschoft-Güttler
(Tübingen); Nathalie Rouquerol (Musée-forum
Aurignac, Frankreich); Helmut Schlaiß – Foto-
grafie (Langenau); Dr. Leif Steguweit (Uni-
versität Erlangen-Nürnberg); Thomas Stephan
(Munderkingen); Dr. Iris Trautmann (München);
Jürgen Werner (Laichingen); Ute Wolf (Stuttgart)

Thomas Beutelspacher, Landesamt für
Denkmalpflege im Regierungspräsidium Stuttgart
(Esslingen)

Michael Bolus, Universität Tübingen,
Heidelberger Akademie der Wissenschaften,
Forschungsstelle "The role of culture in early
expansions of humans" (ROCEEH, Tübingen)

Martha Bright, University of Colorado Springs
(Colorado Springs, USA)

Nicholas J. Conard, Universität Tübingen,
Institut für Ur- und Frühgeschichte und Archäo-
logie des Mittelalters, Abteilung für Ältere
Urgeschichte und Quartärökologie, Senckenberg-
Center for Human Evolution and Paleoecology
(Tübingen)

Frederick L. Coolidge, University of Colorado
Springs (Colorado Springs, USA)

Nicole Ebinger-Rist, Landesamt für
Denkmalpflege im Regierungspräsidium Stuttgart
(Esslingen)

Harald Floss, Universität Tübingen, Institut
für Ur- und Frühgeschichte und Archäologie des
Mittelalters, Abteilung Ältere Urgeschichte
und Quartärökologie (Tübingen)

Wulf Hein (Dorn-Assenheim)

Angela Holdermann (Ranggen, Austria)

Claus-Joachim Kind, Landesamt für
Denkmalpflege im Regierungspräsidium Stuttgart
(Esslingen)

Johannes Krause, Universität Tübingen,
Institut für Naturwissenschaftliche Archäologie,
Arbeitsbereich Archäo- und Paläogenetik
(Tübingen)

Maria Malina, Universität Tübingen,
Heidelberger Akademie der Wissenschaften,
Forschungsstelle "The role of culture in early
expansions of humans" (ROCEEH, Tübingen)

Susanne C. Münzel, Universität Tübingen,
Naturwissenschaftliche Archäologie,
Arbeitsbereich Archäozoologie (Tübingen)

Karenleigh A. Overmann, University of
Oxford, UCCS Center for Cognitive Archaeology
(Oxford, England)

Wolf-Henning Petershagen (Ulm)

Philip Scharer (Stuttgart)

Frank Trommer (Blaubeuren)

Kurt Wehrberger, Ulmer Museum (Ulm)

Johannes Wiedmann, Urgeschichtliches
Museum (Blaubeuren)

Sibylle Wolf, Universität Tübingen, Institut
für Ur- und Frühgeschichte und Archäologie des
Mittelalters, Abteilung Ältere Urgeschichte
und Quartärökologie (Tübingen)

Thomas Wynn, University of Colorado Springs
(Colorado Springs, USA)

Reinhard Ziegler, Staatliches Museum für
Naturkunde/Museum am Löwentor (Stuttgart)

Urgeschichtliches Museum (Blaubeuren)

Wulf Hein – Archäo-Technik (Dorn-Assenheim)

Landesamt für Denkmalpflege im
Regierungspräsidium Stuttgart (Esslingen)

Archäologisches Landesmuseum
Baden-Württemberg (Constance)

Soprintendente per i beni archeologici
del Veneto (Padova, Italy)

Naturkunde- und Mammutmuseum (Siegsdorf)

Landesmuseum Württemberg (Stuttgart)

Staatliches Museum für Naturkunde/
Museum am Löwentor (Stuttgart)

Universität Tübingen, Institut für Ur- und
Frühgeschichte und Archäologie des Mittelalters, Abteilung Ältere Urgeschichte und
Quartärökologie/Museum Schloss Hohen-
tübingen (Tübingen)

Naturhistorisches Museum (Vienna, Austria)

Archäologisches Landesmuseum Baden-Württemberg, Abteilung Ältere Urgeschichte und Quartärökologie der Eberhard Karls Universität Tübingen (Hrsg.) 2010: Eiszeit. Kunst und Kultur. Begleitband zur Großen Landesausstellung 2009/10 Stuttgart. Ostfildern.

Bahn, P. G., Vertut, J. 1997: Journey through the Ice Age. London.

Banerjee, A., Eckmann, C. 2011: Elfenbein und Archäologie. INCENTIVS-Tagungsbeiträge 2004–2007. Römisch-Germanisches Zentralmuseum Mainz. Tagungsbeiträge Bd. 7.

Beutelspacher, T., Kind, C. J. 2012: Auf der Suche nach Fragmenten des Löwenmenschen in der Stadelhöhle im Hohlenstein bei Asselfingen. Archäologische Ausgrabungen in Baden-Württemberg 2011, 66–71.

Beutelspacher, T., Kind, C. J. 2013: Zum Fortgang der Untersuchungen in der Stadelhöhle im Hohlenstein. Archäologische Ausgrabungen in Baden-Württemberg 2012, 89–92.

Boetzkes, M., Schweitzer, I, Vespermann, J. (Hrsg.) 1999: EisZeit. Das große Abenteuer der Naturbeherrschung. Begleitbuch zur Ausstellung Roemer- und Pelizaeus-Museum Hildesheim.

Bolus, M., Conard, N. J., Kandel, A. W. 1999: Grabungen vor dem Hohlenstein im Lonetal, Gemeinden Bissingen und Asselfingen, Alb-Donau-Kreis. Archäologische Ausgrabungen in Baden-Württemberg 1998, 40–47.

Bolus, M. 2004: Der Übergang vom Mittel- zum Jungpaläolithikum in Europa. Eine Bestandsaufnahme unter besonderer Berücksichtigung Mitteleuropas. Germania 82, 1–54.

Bosinski, G. 1987: Die große Zeit der Eiszeitjäger. Europa zwischen 40.000 und 10.000 v. Chr. Jahrbuch des Römisch-Germanischen Zentralmuseums Mainz 34, 3–139.

Bosinski, G. 1990: Homo sapiens. L'histoire des chasseurs du Paléolithique supérieur en Europe. Paris.

Bosinski, G. 2013: Les précurseurs de l'art aurignacien. Mémoire LVI de la Société préhistorique francaise, 497–511.

Clottes, J. 2008: Cave Art. London.

Clottes, J., Lewis-Williams D. 1997, Schamanen. Trance und Magie in der Höhlenkunst der Steinzeit. Sigmaringen.

Coolidge, F., Overmann, K.A. 2012: Numerosity, Abstraction, and the Emergence of Symbolic Thinking. Current Anthropology 53, 204–225.

Combier, J., Jouve, G. 2012: Chauvet cave's art is not Aurignacian: a new examination of the archaeological evidence and dating procedures. Quartär 59, 131–152.

Conard, N. J. 2003: Palaeolithic ivory sculptures from southwestern Germany and the origins of figurative art. Nature 426, 830–832.

Conard, N. J. 2009: A female figurine from the basal Aurignacian of Hohle Fels Cave in southwestern Germany. Nature 459, 248–252.

Conard, N. J., Bolus, M. 2003: Radiocarbon dating and the appearance of modern humans and timing of cultural innovations in Europe: new results and new challenges. Journal of Human Evolution 44, 331–371.

Conard, N. J., Malina, M., Münzel, S. C., Seeberger, F. 2004: Eine Mammutelfenbeinflöte aus dem Aurignacien des Geissenklösterle – Neue Belege für eine musikalische Tradition im frühen Jungpaläolithikum auf der Schwäbischen Alb. Archäologisches Korrespondenzblatt 34, 447–462.

Conard, N. J., Kölbl, S., Schürle, W. 2005: Vom Neandertaler zum modernen Menschen. Ostfildern.

Conard, N. J., Malina, M. 2009: Spektakuläre Funde aus dem unteren Aurignacien vom Hohle Fels bei Schelklingen, Alb-Donau-Kreis. Archäologische Ausgrabungen in Baden-Württemberg 2008, 19–22.

Conard, N. J. et al. 2009: New flutes document the earliest musical tradition in southwestern Germany. Nature 460, 737–740.

Conard, N. J., Kölbl, S. (Hrsg.) 2010: Die Venus vom Hohle Fels. Urgeschichtliches Museum Blaubeuren, Museumsheft 9.

Conard, N. J., Zeidi, M., Bega, J. 2013: Die letzte Kampagne der Nachgrabungen am Vogelherd. Archäologische Ausgrabungen in Baden-Württemberg 2012, 84–88.

Cook, J. 2013: Ice Age art. The arrival of the modern mind. Begleitbuch zur Ausstellung British Museum London.

Dal Magro, G., Zugni-Tauro, A. P. 1992: Auf den Spuren des Löwen. Eine Kunst- und Kulturgeschichte. München.

Delporte, H. 1998: Les Aurignaciens. Premiers hommes modernes. Paris.

Floss, H. 2005: Die Kunst der Eiszeit in Europa. In: Schürle, W., Conard, N. J. (Hrsg.): Zwei Weltalter. Eiszeitkunst und die Bildwelt Willi Baumeisters. Ostfildern-Ruit, 8–69.

Floss, H. 2006: Als der Mensch schuf, schuf er richtig – Europas kreativer Urknall vor 35.000 Jahren. In: Uelsberg, G., Loetters, S., (Hrsg.), Roots, Wurzeln der Menschheit. Begleitbuch zur Ausstellung Rheinisches Landesmuseum Bonn, 209–226.

Floss, H. 2012: Bilder von Leben und Tod – Die Eiszeitkunst. In: Lang, A., Marinkovic, P. (Hrsg.), Bios-Cultus-(Im)mortalitas. Zu Religion und Kultur – von den biologischen Grundlagen bis zu Jenseitsvorstellungen. Internationale Archäologie 16, 87–92.

Floss, H., Rouquerol, N. (Hrsg.) 2007: Les chemins de l'Art aurignacien en Europe – Das Aurignacien und die Anfänge der Kunst in Europa. Colloque International, Aurignac 2005, Éditions Musée-forum Aurignac 4.

Foucault, A., Patou-Mathis, M. (Hrsg.) 2004: Au temps des mammouths. Begleitbuch zur Ausstellung Muséum national d'Histoire naturelle Paris.

Gamble, C. 1999: The Hohlenstein-Stadel revisited. In: Turner, E., Gaudzinski, S. (Hrsg.), The role of early humans in the accumulation of European Lower and Middle Palaeolithic bone assemblages. Monographien des Römisch Germanischen Zentralmuseums Mainz, 305–324.

Hahn, J. 1977: Aurignacien. Das ältere Jungpaläolithikum in Mittel- und Osteuropa. Fundamenta Reihe A, Bd. 9. Köln, Wien.

Hahn, J. 1970: Die Stellung der männlichen Statuette aus dem Hohlenstein-Stadel in der jungpaläolithischen Kunst. Germania 48, 1–12.

Hahn, J. 1992: Eiszeitschmuck auf der Schwäbischen Alb. Ulm.

Hahn, J., Müller-Beck, H., Taute, W. 1985: Eiszeithöhlen im Lonetal. Archäologie einer Landschaft auf der Schwäbischen Alb. Zweite, neubearbeitete und ergänzte Auflage. Stuttgart.

Hahn, J. 1986: Kraft und Aggression. Die Botschaft der Eiszeitkunst im Aurignacien Süddeutschlands? Archaeologica Venatoria 7. Tübingen.

Hahn, J. 1993: Urgeschichtliche Forschung auf der Ostalb. Karst und Höhle, 213–224.

Hansch, W. (Hrsg.), Eiszeit – Mammut, Urmensch und wie weiter? Begleitbuch zur Ausstellung Städtische Museen Heilbronn.

Hein, W., Wehrberger, K. 2010: Löwen- mensch 2.0 – Nachbildung der Elfenbein- statuette aus der Hohlestein-Stadel-Höhle mit authentischen Werkzeugen. In: Experi- mentelle Archäologie in Europa, Bilanz 2010, Heft 9, 47–53.

Higham, T. et al. 2012: Testing models for the beginnings of the Aurignacian and the advent of figurative art and music: The radiocarbon chronology of Geißenklösterle. Journal of Human Evolution 53, 1–13.

Jager, U., Koch, U. (Hrsg.) 1994: Mammuts aus Sibirien. Begleitbuch zur Ausstellung Hessisches Landesmuseum Darmstadt.

Kasten, E. (Hrsg.) 2009: Schamanen Sibiriens. Magier, Mittler, Heiler. Begleitbuch zur Ausstellung Lindenmuseum Stuttgart.

Keller, K. 1986: Sagen aus dem Lonetal. Vaihingen/Enz.

Knecht, H., Pike-Tay, A., White, R. (Hrsg.) 1993: Before Lascaux. The Complex Record of the Early Upper Palaeolithic. Florida.

Kölbl, S., Conard, N.J. (Hrsg.) 2003: Eiszeitschmuck. Status und Schönheit. Urgeschichtliches Museum Blaubeuren. Museumsheft 6.

Lawson, A.J. 2012: Painted caves. Oxford.

Lister, A., Bahn, P. 1997: Mammuts. Die Riesen der Eiszeit. Sigmaringen.

Lorblanchet, M. 1997: Höhlenmalerei. Ein Handbuch. Sigmaringen 1997.

Koenigswald, W.v. 2002: Lebendige Eiszeit. Klima und Tierwelt im Wandel. Darmstadt.

Mikhailova, N. 2006: The cult of the deer and shamans in deer hunting society. Archaeologia Baltica 7, 187–198.

Mohen, J.P. 2002: Arts et Préhistoire. Paris.

Morphy, H. (Hrsg.) 1989: Animals into art. London.

Müller-Beck, H. (Hrsg.) 1983: Urgeschichte in Baden-Württemberg.Stuttgart.

Müller-Beck, H., Albrecht, G. (Hrsg.) 1987: Die Anfänge der Kunst vor 30.000 Jahren. Begleitbuch zur Ausstellung Kunsthalle Tübingen. Stuttgart.

Müller-Beck, H. 1998: Die Steinzeit. Der Weg der Menschen in die Geschichte. München.

Müller-Beck, H. 2011: Lon(e)talforschung von 1931 bis 1941. Wissenschaftliches Projekt – Projekt des NSD-Dozentenbundes an der Wissenschaftlichen Akademie Tübingen – ab 1935 unter Schirmherrschaft des Reichsführers SS Heinrich Himmler, in: Schallmeyer, E., Kurzynski, K. v. (Hrsg.): Archäologie und Politik. Archäologische Ausgrabungen der 30er und 40er Jahre des 20. Jahrhunderts im zeitgenössischen Kontext. Fundberichte aus Hessen, Beiheft 7, 121–140.

Müller-Beck, H., Conard, N.J., Schürle, W. (Hrsg.) 2001: Eiszeitkunst im süddeutsch-schweizerischen Jura. Stuttgart.

Orschiedt, J. 1999: Manipulationen an menschlichen Skelettresten. Taphonomische Prozesse, Sekundärbestattungen oder Kannibalismus? Urgeschichtliche Material-hefte Bd. 13. Tübingen.

Piprani, J. 2011: Material Culture, Behaviour, and Identity: The Human Body as Experiential Nexus. Time and Mind vol 4 issue 3, 325–336.

Porr, M. 2010: Palaeolithic Art as Cultural Memory: a Case Study of the Aurignacian Art of Southwest Germany. Cambridge Archaeological Journal 20:1, 87–108.

Probst, E. 2009: Höhlenlöwen. Raubkatzen im Eiszeitalter. Norderstedt.

Riek, G. 1934: Die Eiszeitjägerstation am Vogelherd im Lonetal. Bd. 1, Die Kulturen. Tübingen.

Ryan, R.E. 1999: The strong eye of shamanism. A Journey into the caves of consciouness, Rochester/Vermont.

Scharer, P. 2010: Robert F. Wetzel (1898–1962). Anatom, Urgeschichtler, National-sozialist. Inaugural-Dissertation zur Erlangung des Doktorgrades der Zahn-heilkunde der Medizinischen Fakultät der Eberhard-Karls-Universität zu Tübingen.

Scheer, A. (Hrsg.) 1995: Eiszeitwerkstatt. Experimentelle Archäologie. Urgeschichtliches Museum Blaubeuren. Museumsheft 2.

Schmid, E. 1989: Die altsteinzeitliche Elfenbeinstatuette aus der Höhle Stadel im Hohlenstein bei Asselfingen, Alb-Donau-Kreis. Fundberichte aus Baden-Württem-berg 14, 33–96.

Steguweit, L. (Hrsg.) 2008: Menschen der Eiszeit. Jäger, Handwerker, Künstler. Begleitbuch zur Ausstellung Stadtmuseum Erlangen.

Ulmer Museum (Hrsg.) 1994: Der Löwen-mensch. Tier und Mensch in der Kunst der Eiszeit. Begleitbuch zur Ausstellung Ulmer Museum. Sigmaringen.

Vialou, D. 1991: La Préhistoire. Paris.

Werner, J. 2010: Spurensuche auf der Schwäbischen Alb. Bad Schussenried.

Wetzel, R. 1961: Der Hohlestein im Lonetal. Dokumente alteuropäischer Kulturen vom Eiszeitalter bis zur Völkerwanderung. Mitteilungen des Vereins für Naturwissen-schaft und Mathematik in Ulm (Donau) 26, 21–75.

Wiesing, U., Brintzinger, K.R., Grün, B., Junginger, H., Michl, S. (Hrsg.) 2010: Die Universität Tübingen im Nationalsozia-lismus. Contubernium. Tübinger Beiträge zur Universitäts- und Wissenschaftsgeschichte Bd. 73. Stuttgart.

pp. 2–3 Greeting and foreword: Landesamt für Denkmalpflege im RP Stuttgart,
T. Beutelspacher, Y. Mühleis.

pp. 8–19 Wehrberger: 1 from Bürger, L.
1892: Der Bockstein, das Fohlenhaus, der
Salzbühl, drei prähistorische Wohnstätten
im Lonethal. Mitteilungen des Vereins
für Kunst und Altertum in Ulm und Ober-
schwaben Heft 3; **2** from Adam, K.D. 1972/
73: Anfänge urgeschichtlichen Forschens
in Südwestdeutschland. Quartär 23/24,
21–36, portrait by history painter Carl
Häberlin, Stuttgart; **3, 8, 9, 21, 22** Universität Tübingen; **4** from Fraas, O. 1872: Beiträge zur Kulturgeschichte aus schwäbischen
Höhlen entnommen. Archiv für Anthropo-
logie 5; **5** Ulmer Museum; **6** J. Wiedmann;
7 from Riek 1934; **10** Landesamt für Denkmalpflege Baden-Württemberg, O. Braasch;
11–14 Ulmer Museum, diary R. Wetzel;
15 from Südwest Presse 3.6.2013;
16 T. Stephan; **17** copy Universität Tübingen,
M. Zeidi (modified); **18–20, 23** Universität
Tübingen, H. Jensen; **24** Universität
Tübingen, M. Malina; **25** J. Lipták.

pp. 20–25 Wehrberger: 1, 2, 4, 5, 7 Ulmer
Museum, diary R. Wetzel; **3** Title-page
Wetzel, R. et al. 1941: Die Lontalforschung.
Plan und Zwischenbericht. Jahresbände
der wissenschaftlichen Akademie Tübingen
des NSD-Dozentenbundes; **6** H. Schlaiß.

pp. 28–35 Wehrberger: 1, 2, 8, 11 Ulmer
Museum, diary R. Wetzel; **3** W. Adler;
4 Text from Keller 1986; **5** Max Planck
Institut Leipzig, J. Krause; **6** Ulmer Museum;
7 from Ratsprotokoll Stadtarchiv Ulm 1591;
9, 10 J. Orschiedt; 12 after Wetzel 1938;
13–15 Landesamt für Denkmalpflege
im RP Stuttgart, T. Beutelspacher;

16 Ulmer Museum; **17** Title-page Wetzel, R.,
Gieseler, W. 1938: Die Kopfbestattung und
die Knochentrümmerstätte des Hohlensteins im Rahmen der Urgeschichte des
Lonetals, Anthropologischer Bericht über
die Kopfbestattung und die Knochentrümmerstätte des Hohlensteins im Lonetal.
Verhandlungen der Deutschen Gesellschaft
für Rassenforschung 9.

pp. 36–41 Wehrberger: 1, 4 Ulmer
Museum, diary R. Wetzel; **2, 3, 5, 7** Ulmer
Museum; **6** private photo; **8–10** Landesmuseum Württemberg, Stuttgart;
11 K. H. Augustin (Esslingen).

pp. 44–51 Kind: 1 J. Werner; **2–4, 6–8,
10–13** Landesamt für Denkmalpflege im RP
Stuttgart; **5** Ulmer Museum; **9** H. Schlaiß;
14 Bundesarchiv Berlin Document Center
NS 19/1295.

**pp. 52–61 Ebinger-Rist, Wolf: 1, 3–14,
15** Landesamt für Denkmalpflege im RP
Stuttgart, Y. Mühleis, **2** C. v. Elm.

**pp. 64–73 Ebinger-Rist et al.:
1–12** Landesamt für Denkmalpflege im RP
Stuttgart, Y. Mühleis; **13** C. v. Elm.

pp. 74–77 Bolus: 1 from Verna, C.,
Dujardin, V., Trinkaus, E. 2012, The Early
Aurignacian human remains from La
Quina-Aval (France). Journal of Human
Evolution 62, 605–617; **2** from Trinkaus,
E. 2010, Denisova Cave, Peştera cu Oase,
and Human Divergence in the Late Pleisto-
cene. PaleoAnthropology, 196–200; **3, 5**
Universität Tübingen, H. Jensen; **4** from
Lartet, E. 1861, Nouvelles recherches sur
la coexistence de l'homme et des grands
mammifères fossiles réputés caractéris-
tiques de la dernière période géologique.
Annales des Sciences naturelles.
II. Zoologie, 4ème série, XV, 177–253.

pp. 80–89 Floss: 1, 6, 7 Universität
Tübingen, H. Jensen; **2, 3** Universität
Tübingen, **4** copy Universität Tübingen
(modified); **5** Landesamt für Denkmalpflege im RP Stuttgart, C.J. Kind;
8 Universität Tübingen, M. Malina.

pp. 90–95 Wolf: 1 Universität Tübingen,
M. Malina; **2, 4–6** Universität Tübingen,
H. Jensen, S. Wolf, mounting G. Häussler;
3 Universität Tübingen, H. Jensen

pp. 98–103 Münzel, Conard: 1 Universität
Tübingen, H. Jensen; **2–4** J. Lipták;
5, 6 S. C. Münzel, Workshop Federsee-
museum 2006.

pp. 106–109 Wehrberger: 1 Landesamt
für Denkmalpflege im RP Stuttgart,
T. Beutelspacher; **2** B. Alexander –
ArcticPhoto.

pp. 110–115 Wolf: 1 Naturkunde- und
Mammutmuseum Siegsdorf, R. Darga;
2 Museum d'Histoire Naturelle de la Ville
d'Autun; **3** Staatliches Museum für Natur-
kunde/Museum am Löwentor, Stuttgart,
A. Lehmkuhl; **4** Universität Tübingen,
H. Jensen; **5** after R. White (1995); **6** Ulmer
Museum; **7, 8** Universität Tübingen,
R. Ehmann; **9** Hermitage, St. Petersburg;
10 J. Lipták; **11, 12** F. Trommer.

pp. 118–125 Ziegler: 1 Staatliches
Museum für Naturkunde/Museum am
Löwentor, painting by R. Kiwit, photo
H. Lumpe; **2, 3** Staatliches Museum für
Naturkunde/Museum am Löwentor,
R. Harling; **4** from Goldfuss, G.A. 1810:
Die Umgebung von Muggendorf. Ein
Taschenbuch für Freunde der Natur- und
Altertumskunde. Erlangen; **5** J. Reiter,
www.foto-chiemgau.de; **6–10** Universität
Tübingen, S. C. Münzel.